To LEE.

THIS IS f

The Best Gift Ever

For: <u>My Favorite Sailor</u>

SPECIAL. NOT ME. I
JUST WROTE. IT.

Volume One

Tim

Tim Tunks

ISBN-10

1492325449

ISBN-13:

978-1492325444

DEDICATION

This book is dedicated to my amazing wife Debby,
Without whom, where would I be?
And the talented Donna Ikkanda who gets credit for all the book
sales to buyers who judge a book by its cover,
And my friend and publisher Pat Reynolds and my other literary
friends Dick Ward, Tom Fenske,
Dr. Michael Glock, Marvin Mudrick,
And all the others who've influenced my literary development.

Special thanks to all my sailing mentors:
Hank McGill, Dusty Way, Charlie O'Leary, and all the rest.

And a special thank you to Michael Morris and
Jennifer Silva Redmond;
You have provided priceless help.

Thank you all.

Introduction

Throughout history, sailors have learned the joys of understanding nature in a special way. For sailors, nature is their quite literal engine of propulsion, as central to their purpose as the motors in their automobiles, but available for a far more intimate relationship. Much of this book comes from my decade sailing and living off the grid along Mexico's western coast, but the imaginative reader will easily see additional applications for information gleaned from these pages.

Sailing is the best gift I've ever received, because it has brought me so many other gifts.

Topping that list is my appreciation for mentoring and those who do it. My good fortune at having my friend Hank introduce me to this wind -powered world has blazed a path I've followed ever since—encountering several priceless mentors along the way and becoming a mentor myself.

This book is a package made from the gifts my mentors have gifted me, and it is my gift to you.

You are fortunate to have the friend who bought it.

CONTENTS

The Self-Sufficient Sailor

Racing

Tips, Tools and Techniques

End Note - Passing It On

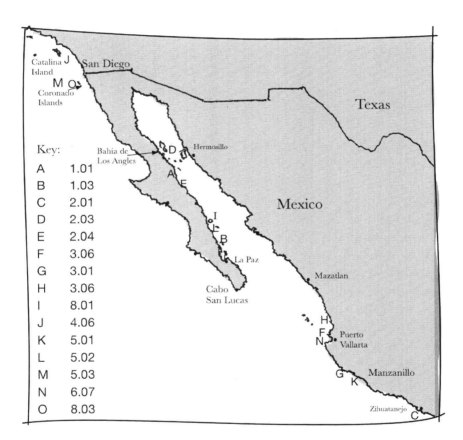

Many of the following stories take place at locales along the Pacific coast of Mexico and north into the Sea of Cortez

Ships are the nearest thing to dreams that hands have ever made.

THE STORY BEGINS

The following story of dolphin births happened about halfway through my forty-year romance with sailing. I chose it as an example of the intimacy one feels with nature when sailing is your mode of transport and your vessel is your home.

There is a special community of sailors that seems similar in all the parts of the world I know. We all seem to be curious independent folks relishing the discoveries we make and the inventions we create as we practice our craft. It is this curiosity and joy of discovery that I wish to celebrate.

[1.01] It Takes a Pod

"It takes a village to raise a child" became a popular slogan in the 1990s, which was my decade aboard *Scallywag*, sailing in the warm waters of Western Mexico. This saying was well known in both Native American and African cultures well before Hilary Clinton picked it up.

I witnessed a drama that expressed this message in a most unexpected manner, and it is there that I begin my story of discovery.

The stage was set in a beautiful little bay called Bahia San Francisquito on the peninsular coast of the Sea of Cortez. About sixty miles south of Bahia de Los Angeles, this calm body of water with its narrow entrance and sandy beaches is a popular birthing center for dolphins. This was something I didn't know until I witnessed it early one morning while serenely anchored enjoying a morning coffee.

Like many events that unfold before our eyes, the significance of what transpired revealed itself gradually. With the "stage" about 150 yards away, powerful binoculars gave a good view of the performance without influencing the action.

The prologue was an unusual grouping of Common Dolphins milling about near the beach. Suddenly three juveniles began a series of exuberant leaps and spins into the air. These acrobats performed to announce each birth, giving us first one encore and then another to announce the third pup's birth. The juveniles were like the teenagers you sometimes see at family picnics, weddings, and other gatherings. They seem to be serving the needs of the event while really amusing themselves with their own private games.

From my reference books onboard I learned the birthing mother was generally accompanied by two or more "aunts" who stayed close by to assist if required. The juveniles swim about at a respectful distance, keeping a watchful eye for any approaching dangers while the rest of the pod seems to doze, swimming in slow motion and surfacing for a lazy breath now and then — until the pod was alerted by the suddenly leaping youngsters.

In the next act of this dolphin drama, adults nosed the calves to the surface from time to time, helping them get the rhythm of breathing and swimming as the ensemble repeatedly paralleled the beach. The calves were "drafted" along between the adults, just as my old VW Microbus driven close behind fast-moving trucks got sucked along for better efficiency on highway trips.

Witnessing such an intimate scene colored the rest of my day, and I chose to remain there at anchor until the next morning.

That second morning I witnessed a remedial swimming lesson for one pup, who, for whatever reasons, had not gained sufficient skill from his first day's efforts. The pup's mother and mentors patiently repeated yesterday's lessons, for the pod cannot depart until the newest members have sufficient swimming skill to tuck into the slipstreams and be carried along in the flow of their extended family. It seemed the extra tutoring took hold after a bit and this village regrouped and swam together out of the bay—off to their aquatic life of feeding, resting, birthing, playing, and defending their group from dangers.

I became nostalgic for my early youth lived in the 1950s mid-western U.S. where we were all members of the same tightly-knit family looking after one another.

You may be certain this experience had a profound effect on me. Perhaps this is why I am ready, nowadays, to apply a bit of mentoring when I see the need.

"It takes a pod to raise a pup." seems to be the apt takeaway, and giving thanks for the opportunity to witness such an intimate event is part of my mission in writing this book.

With a fine sailing vessel and the grand good fortune to have a decade to sail it about Mexico waters, I made a huge catalogue of discoveries, many of which will be shared in these pages. Imagination and invention were ever-present elements in those discoveries and will be celebrated in the stories to follow.

[1.02] Curiosity and Discovery

It took me nearly two decades of preparation to sail into that little Baja California bay for there was much to learn about sailing, much to learn about boats and their systems, and much to learn about me.

The sport of yacht racing teaches sailors a wealth of sailing and seamanship skills while it collects a most interesting and diverse community. Within this community are many generous mentors who help build and unite our diverse group. Many of the stories, inventions, and techniques you will find in the following pages are drawn from racing's lessons.

Another large sailing subgroup are the cruising sailors, a few of whom, like me, have racing in their DNA. You will find tales within these covers of what can happen in the crossover territory where racing and cruising meet. I've had some of my best fun mixing racing and cruising experiences.

Sailors' natural curiosity and sense of adventure lead them to discover new experiences. These discoveries are the lessons that teach the self-sufficiency sailors seek. Both success and failure have their lessons, so embrace them both.

You will read how I learned many of my lessons and may be surprised to discover how many of them I learned through the process of teaching others.

Mentorship is a time-consuming process and it seems the more technologically advanced we become (preoccupied with our time saving devices) the less time we have for this rewarding activity. I celebrate mentorship within these pages, imagining what we now have, overlaid with what we can have in the future.

For much of my middle-age phase I had imagined I'd end up one of those crusty old bachelor types you'd see living aboard an old boat that is in a constant process of restoration. On the dock, in the boatyard, or in the yacht club bar I'd have answers to most questions nautical and some that were philosophical or spiritual. The universe needs such people and I felt I could perform that role as well as anyone. 'Twas only a fortunate act of fate that led me onto my present path where I write stories in my Santa Monica nest with two loyal cats and one fine spouse.

As I'm not a fixture on your dock or in your club and I now stay away from boatyards, I'm delivering lessons learned and discoveries I've made in this gift book. Much of this volume is a celebration of curiosity pursued and sensitivities gained through my sailing experiences.

[1.03] Happy Story with a Sad Ending

Los Islotes is a large rocky structure protruding above the water just north of Isla Partida, thirty miles or so north of La Paz, B.C.S. Mexico. However, it is below the water that you experience the charm and wonder of the place. Los Islotes is the birthing spot and the playground for a colony of Lobos del Mar—Sea Lions in English.

What is most wonderful is how closely humans and sea mammals interact here!

This playground was a favorite spot that I would visit and share with others dozens of times during my decade cruising Mexico on *Scallywag*, my 37-foot Islander Sloop. Only a half hour's dinghy ride from protected anchorages, Islotes was a favorite day trip when winds were calm. At midday, pangas with 175-horsepower outboard engines would arrive from La Paz, unload a batch of freshly pink-skinned snorkel-breathing tourists to splash about for an hour or so, and then reload and thankfully depart.

But many visits remained private audiences with my 10 foot inflatable dinghy, *Sweet Mona*, the only vessel in sight. It was one of those private times that provided the following set of experiences I will never forget.

There were only two of us in this party, and it was the first visit for her. I had been there many times before, so I was familiar with the behaviors and customs of Islotes society.

First, there was no hunting in this preserve, for human predators would be immediately recognized as a challenge and a threat to the resident critter society. On entering the water with fins, mask and snorkel, one or two large males would come quite close to greet you and sniff out your intent. Your proper response was to act shy and look away with the attitude of a small child holding her mother's skirt in the face of loud advancing relatives. When they were certain you were not a threat, they'd go off about their business of fishing, or sleeping, or harassing their harems.

The juveniles were the next arrivals. They would zoom by the humans at top speed, turning on a dime and diving in a corkscrew spiral only to jet up again to the surface. All this happened under the watchful eyes of the nearby mothers. Etiquette required another shy performance from us to reassure the moms, which when properly performed released the guarding parents to retire and relax a watchful distance away.

The relaxing mothers were some kind of signal to the juveniles that these humans are approved playmates, and they would come quite close to look into your face and sometimes nip at a diver's swim fin to sample its taste. My routine to engage them in play was to hover like an inverted post about ten feet below the surface, and then to spin around a couple of times when I was certain I had their attention. The immediate group reaction was something akin to "Is that all you got?"

"Check this out, Dude!" they would seem to say as they began their own amazing gymnastic aerial underwater performance.

This play could continue until they either got bored or over-excited, like puppies who switched from playful dodging and lunging to snarling and biting. Either way, this was the signal to the humans that it was time to move on.

The next stop on the tour was a swim right up to the rocks, with another shy display, to observe the population hauled out in the warm sun to sleep or socialize. There were a few very young pups nursing, but the most stirring sight was a newborn who looked like a barely moving seal skin bag of bones with his mother licking away the gleaming placenta. What a wonder to be that close to such a monumental and intimate event!

But this day still had much to offer. These first events were in the rocky shallow water south of the major outcropping. Our next stop was reached by a swim through a narrow surging passage to the north deep side, where the rocks formed a steep underwater cliff reaching down more than 150 feet. There is a strong deep water current that is interrupted and diverted by Los Islotes, and this is where fish come to fish. The tuna seems to be the top predator here, swooping through occasional schools of Jack Cravalle, who would in turn be feeding on smaller species.

Our observation of lunchtime at this aquatic cafeteria was interrupted when Elvis arrived and challenged our right to be there.

Who is this "Elvis," you might well ask, as did I when I first heard about him and his infamous reputation. He was a young adult elephant seal who weighed around 800 pounds, and he was the only elephant seal around. Naturally, he was used to getting his way, having more than four times the mass of the next largest mammals around.

He was regarded as an unwelcome visitor by the Mexican Tourist Bureau, and they even went so far as to get the Marine Institute to capture him once, and transport him to the nearest elephant seal colony nearly 500 miles away at Cedros Island in the Pacific near Turtle Bay. Elvis had just recently returned and was begging for another capture.

His aggressive adolescent male hormones drove him to fatal amorous attacks on poor young female sea lions, and he even once went after a female marine biologist scuba diver, grabbing her and diving to 50 feet with her in his lusty embrace. The young woman was very lucky that she had both scuba and moxie, for without either, she would surely have perished.

So here was Elvis telling us to get the hell out of his yard and off his grass, and I was quite willing to go. My companion, however, knew nothing of Elvis, his history, or his habits, and felt that she should stand up to him and face him down as a brave dog whisperer might do with a snarling mutt. We were separated by too great a distance for me to effectively communicate that a less confrontational approach was definitely advisable.

When playing with the pups, they would sometimes come and bark right in your face making a little sound behind a cloud of bubbles. Elvis had a similar technique, but his was orders of magnitude more intimidating. The force of his bubble cloud could be felt, along with the resonance of his loud bark, which set me back considerably. After Elvis repeated this warning to my companion, she got the idea and we made a discreet exit back through the passage, leaving Elvis to find other amusements.

But now we are approaching the sad ending I warned you about.

While swimming along the south edge of the rocks back to where the *Sweet Mona* was anchored, we were met by a small delegation of three adults escorting one young pup who was wearing a collar of four-inch diameter pipe that had very rough flame cut edges—which was tragically cutting into his fleshy neck!

Clearly this delegation was asking for assistance they knew was unlikely to be rendered, and they were effective in shaming us deeply for belonging to the race that left such a dangerous toy lying about. What guilt I felt at watching a death sentence being slowly executed!

So there is the sad ending, which reminds me of birds with plastic six-pack collars, and fish with plastic in their stomachs, and finless shark carcasses washed up on the beaches and all the other horrors we mindlessly unleash. Perhaps the happy parts of this story might help to communicate the value of a mindfulness towards all life forms—including our own.

A sure cure for seasickness? Stand under a tree.

[1.04] Snorkel Hiking

Snorkeling around the warm Pacific waters of Mexico was like taking private nature hikes through wildlife-populated scenic wilderness—only these hikes explored an underwater countryside. As life aboard *Scallywag* was living "off the Grid," nature played a central role in daily life, with hardly a day going by without at least one swimming expedition.

Some swims were multi-tasking endeavors. For instance it was my custom to keep a loaded speargun dangling from a line astern when I'd dive to wipe the little sea critters off *Scallywag's* bottom. The fresh load of food that floated off from my bottom cleaning would attract feeding small fish, and the arrival of small fish was generally followed by the arrival of larger fish, many of whom became delightful dinner companions.

A pole-spear or speargun was a common accessory for a snorkeling hike because one never knew when a likely meal would present itself, but snorkeling unarmed provided additional opportunities. As I learned to spearfish it became obvious how differently sea life reacted when I was hunting compared to when I was just sightseeing unarmed. Most of the truly tasty fish eat fish themselves, and are, in their turn, potential meals for larger fish. These fish were both predators and prey, so they knew how to recognize hunting when they saw it.

As rewarding as I found being a successful hunter-gatherer, my most rewarding underwater encounters have not been on hunting expeditions.

2

NATURAL WONDERS

[2.01] Regular Morning Swim with Ray

Zihuatanejo is a classic sleepy Mexican seaside resort, popular since the middle of the last century.   Located on its own beautiful bay in the southern state of Guerrero, it has become a popular winter anchorage for many international cruising boats.   The high-rise hotels and the modern marina located in Ixtapa a few miles up the coast seem to skim off many of the luxury-seeking loud partying tourists, which helped make Zihuatanejo my favorite place to anchor for a month or two each winter.

The northern part of Zihuatanejo's bay is somewhat protected and adjoins the center of the town with its beach, where fishermen sort and sell their catch, and cruisers land their dinghies. This anchorage is the most protected so boats swing on a single anchor here, intermixed with fishing pangas and cruising boats of every description.

Next to the inner city anchorage is Playa de Madera (wooden beach in English) with a flat bottom extending from the beach that is perfect for swimming but too shallow for anchoring.

Around a rocky point with fine hotels and a few expensive homes overlooking the the bay is wide La Ropa Beach which looks straight out the bay at the winter sunsets over the open water beyond. This was my favorite spot since fewer cruisers tolerated the longer dinghy ride to town and the necessity of anchoring bow and stern to keep the boat pointing into the swells that entered the wide bay directly from the southwest. I considered it so much my home that I'd set out my anchors and rode with floats like it was a permanent mooring, permitting me to drop my lines and go out for a day sail or a fishing trip and return to my same spot—

usually without fuss unless some other vessel decided my set-up was for their convenience.

My spot was at the far southern end of the beach, which also was the edge of the good holding ground. The bottom south of my spot was mostly oyster-covered smooth rock, impervious to the piercing grip of an anchor and ensuring that *Scallywag's* port side was neighbor-free. Although this position produced some additional privacy it also made *Scallywag* the "turning mark" around which rented jet skis and parasail-towing runabouts would do their 180 degree turns to re-pass along the beach.

One afternoon one of the parasail towing boats lost power after just completing his turn, wrapping the towline around *Scallywag's* mast and unceremoniously dunking a grandmotherly tourist into the water a few feet from our boat. After I'd pulled her into our inflatable dinghy where the runabout retrieved her, the driver asked for the return of his towrope which I denied until I could examine the wind instrument cluster on the masthead for damage with my binoculars.

First he tugged on the towline and I tugged back. Then he braced for a stronger tug as I took a couple of turns around a cockpit winch. After he and his boat had been winched in a few yards, he yielded the contest and waited while I reassured myself there was no damage aloft. That was merely one of the entertainments Playa La Ropa offered.

However it was my good friend Ray who made me feel most at home.

With small restaurants spread along the beach a short swim away serving a fine breakfast of huevos al gusto, frijoles, tortillas, jugo, y cafe (two eggs, beans, tortillas, juice, and coffee) for under three dollars including a good tip, my morning habit was to swim around for forty-five minutes or so with fins, mask, and snorkel before going ashore for breakfast.

My second winter there I met Ray during my morning swim, and he kept me company for nearly half an hour as we swam and dove checking out the anchors of other boats and the quantity of oysters populating the rocky areas of the mostly sandy bottom. Ray was a small brown spotted ray nearly a yard wide from wing tip to wing tip who was both social and acrobatic, swimming in graceful loops from surface to ocean floor. Sometimes he'd slow his normal leisurely pace even more, so that I could follow his arc as he dove and spiraled about.

A pair of intrusive jet skis buzzing by disturbed Ray enough so that we parted company and I went ashore for a fine breakfast and a glowing memory of that intimate half hour we had swum together.

Imagine my joy the next morning when Ray met me shortly after I splashed into the warm water, and we repeated our tour of the anchorage together, not parting ways until my desire for breakfast, and a bit of fatigue from keeping up with Ray, drove me to the beach.

A few minutes into my next morning's swim with Ray, we picked up another most interesting little companion, a tiny yellow fish with black bar stripes up and down both sides. No more than an inch and a quarter long and with a tiny tail that seemed to oscillate faster than a hummingbird's wings, this fish swam unshakably just a few inches in front of my nose. I could surface to look around for traffic, and as soon as my face was back in the water my little fish would regain his station.

We must have been an odd trio with the tiny fish pushed ahead of my faceplate by the pressure wave as we swam about wherever Ray led us. It was certainly odd to me but it also felt hugely rewarding.

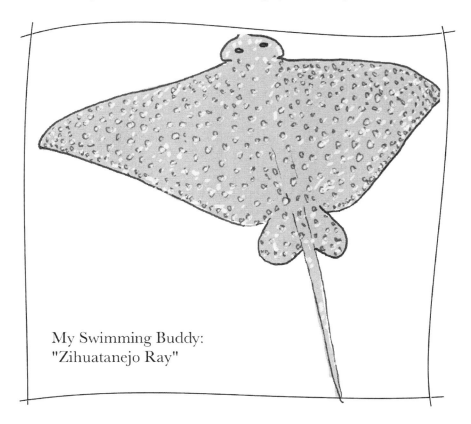

My Swimming Buddy:
"Zihuatanejo Ray"

[2.02] Life at Isla Smith

Strangely named Isla Smith is the largest island in the mouth of Bahia de Los Angeles about a third of the way down the Baja peninsula on the gulf side. About ten miles to the east is Isla Angel de la Guarda, which is nearly thirty miles long and provides some protection to the bay and its nearby islands from easterly weather. This area is fairly remote by land, and nearly 35 miles from the nearest Pemex gas station, with just a small village that supports a fishing fleet and some tourist sport-fishing. It is also the home of an established black sea turtle breeding operation at Camp Archelon that has helped greatly in re-establishing a decimated population. The islands are all uninhabited and now protected as part of a national marine park.

Isla Smith had three of my favorite anchorages in the entire Sea of Cortez, each with its own special feature.

Near the southern tip of the island there is a little protected bay just large enough for a pair of boats friendly to one another. Just a few minutes ride away (in a planing dinghy) is the end of the island, filled with rocky structure and fed by strong tidal currents. To the underwater hunter-gatherer this means good food in the form of lobster, rock scallops, and fish.

Just around the corner on the north side is a narrow rocky inlet, less than a dozen feet wide that opens up into a large shallow tidal lagoon that nearly bisects the island. This is the birthing ground and nursery for the densest ray population I've ever encountered, requiring a shuffling walk along the bottom to reduce the chances of stepping down on a very painful stinger. You could watch the rays shooting out in all directions, with various sized rays distributed at different depths in the sandy bottom. With the largest ones buried deepest in the sand, their size and depth make for more displaced sand and therefore a larger underwater sand explosion when they were spooked from their slumber.

The grand prize of this lagoon was revealed at low tide when a gatherer with a bucket and a pry iron could harvest his fill of the oysters that covered the surrounding rocks. We took a five-gallon bucket once and for days oysters were a feature of most meals; from oyster omelets in the morning to barbecued oysters for lunch, oysters on the half shell for cocktail hour, and baked oysters with dinner. Slung overboard on the shady side of the boat in a burlap sack they were kept happily alive until called to the table.

Toward the north end of the island lies a shallow sandy area protected by a hook of land that looks as if it was built by the hand of man, which it wasn't.   In this sandy shallow lives a large population of delicious clams, so dense that my usual clamming gear included a beach chair and umbrella, along with the clam bucket and the ice chest. The routine was to plant the chair and umbrella in a couple of feet of water, and to then plant yourself in the chair as you dug about on either side with your hands until your harvest rate declined, at which time you'd relocate a few yards away, open a cold one from the ice chest and dig around some more.

Another thing you should know about this wonderful part of Baja California is that the summer is the best time to be there but it can be awfully hot if you're not underwater for much of the day. This is where Isla Smith really shines.

A feature of this narrow island is the volcanic cone that rises several hundred feet above the sea and interrupts the prevailing breeze as it blows west from the mainland. If we had our science teacher handy, we could have an elegant explanation of how air cools as it rises to go over the top of the cone and cools a bit more as it decompresses while rolling down the other side, providing some of nature's own air conditioning. This anchorage is sometimes five to ten degrees cooler than the surrounding area.

The third anchorage I favored is tucked between another tiny island and Isla Smith, just a bit south of the clamming beach. There is good protection when the wind reverses and blows from the west and there are lots of rocky nooks and crannies to explore from the water.   These features make this protected area a popular place for sea critters too, and this is where I met my *lobo del mar*, spanish for wolf of the sea or sea lion to us.

Like my friend Ray in Zihuatanejo, Lobo became a swimming partner.   But unlike Ray, who was there waiting for me when I entered the water, Lobo swam up to the boat and barked impatiently at me to come out for a swim. This was not something I understood at first. Why was this sea lion so close to the boat barking so insistently?   Even after I decided he wanted me in the water I wasn't sure for what purpose. These animals have sharp teeth and swimming strength far exceeding my own.

With a bit of tightness in my nether regions, I gathered fins, mask and snorkel, trying to decide if I should strap on the knife I was used to having at my calf to harvest any rock scallop I might meet. Opting to go unarmed as a gesture of friendliness, I entered the water and enjoyed an unmatched experience of having another creature so consciously showing me his domain.

Reflecting on this experience the next morning I was amazed to hear the same impatient barking next to the boat, so I quickly donned my gear and went for my second, and, as it turned out to be, my last swim with Lobo.

However, there was so much other sea life in my back yard tucked in among the rocks and islets that I did not miss Lobo after he left.

This was early in the summer and the area had just completed its transformation from spring when the winter vegetation has died and become grazing fodder for the large schools of hatchlings who sometimes swam in schools fifty feet wide and more than a block long. These small fish would vacuum the water column of the little fragments of underwater plant life, transforming the cloudy liquid into a gin-clear substance.

There were several different species of baby fish; their size varying from finger length to nearly a foot long, and each school fed at a slightly different depth. Swimming within one of these schools surrounded by so many fish that both the surface and the bottom were obscured was a most amazing experience.

The first time I swam in a school I wondered how they would react if spooked a bit. Like a bratty kid thumping a fish bowl to watch the goldfish jump, I made an underwater bark which made the school twitch and contract as if it was muscle tissue reacting to an electric shock. As punishment for my childish prank, all the fish pooped simultaneously, clouding the water with their output. Luckily, these same fish regarded the material as nourishing food—it had only been eaten once—and the water cleared again as if by magic.

Another day while schooling with the fish, I swam through a traffic intersection that allowed three different schools of three different species to flow through like it was a well designed three-level freeway overpass. I was reminded of John Steinbeck's wonder at seeing the quantity and variety of species on a 1941 expedition to collect specimens which was recorded so brilliantly in his *Log of the Sea of Cortez*.

Give a man a fish and he'll eat for a day.
Teach him to fish and he will disappear for long periods
with a cooler full of beer.

[2.03] The Food Chain Display

One morning we weighed our anchor and headed into the bay to re-provision at the village in Bahia Los Angeles.

Just after clearing our rocky anchorage we had a clear view of the point that protects the bay from the south and saw great numbers of seabirds circling a spot in the sea. We changed course and sailed down to investigate, because we knew that birds in the air meant fish in the sea.

The scene that evolved was only revealed in stages with the final picture completed just as the action climaxed.

Isla Angel de La Guardia narrows the Sea of Cortez at that point, which increases tidal flow rate, like a nozzle on a hose, causing strong currents as the tide floods and drains the gulf to the north. There are also deep underwater canyons, the cracks left when the peninsular land mass broke away from mainland Mexico. The currents circulate food down to the depths where krill, squid, and other species thrive, and then, in turn, those currents upwell the squid and krill for those near the surface to feed upon.

Great quantities of fish come to feed in these food-rich waters—rising to the surface with such force and flow that you can see upwell mounds on the water surface as pronounced as a pitcher's mound.

This time the smaller bait fish were the first to arrive. Soon larger fish herded the baitfish into balls to provide a more concentrated target to feed upon, and these balls of fish boiled the surface, attracting the birds.

The first birds we'd spotted began to feed on the baitfish that hit the surface. With this feeding frenzy now widely advertised by the smaller birds noisy presence, flocks of pelicans arrived, flying in long lines as if they were a train, and dove in scooping up both the baitfish and those fish dining upon them. With all this action in the water, it was not long before the tuna arrived to dart through the melee eating their fill.

With all the birds and fish feeding, the water had become littered with bits of fish that missed the mouths of the diners and the smallest seabirds gathered on the surface to eat their fill.

Something you should know about tuna is that they are rarely found in quantity without the company of dolphins, and the dolphins were soon to arrive. By now the feeding was so confused that we could not see who was eating who or what, but the various species had certainly worked it out on their own.

The climax of this show was the arrival of two large Orcas, sleek black with their white markings, to join the feast. Before long the show was over. Perhaps it was the killer whales who broke it up but we could not tell. First the water stopped boiling with the baitfish and then the pelicans departed. Finally it was only a few of the smallest seabirds who continued to search about for dinner scraps, and then they were gone.

As we anchored in the roadstead in front of the village, we could see another large gathering of birds on the horizon and imagined an encore of the drama we had witnessed.

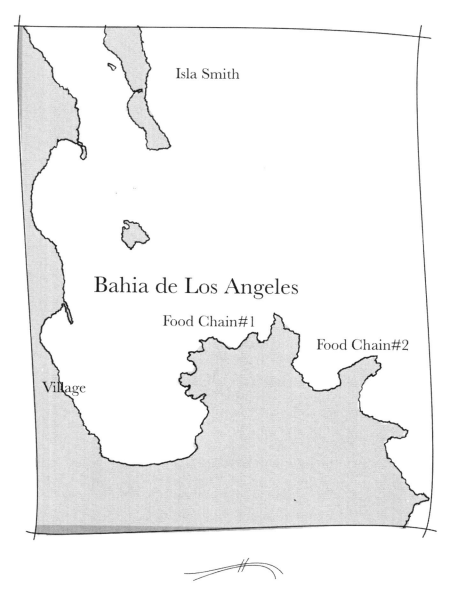

[2.04] Pelican Piracy at Las Animas

Eating from the sea is a combination of fishing, gathering, and hunting, which is spearfishing in our case. This is a story about hunting and spearfishing.

First let me disabuse the squeamish among my readers of the notion that spearfishing is more brutal than line fishing. With spearfishing you only take the fish you choose for eating, never catching the wrong size or species that must be returned to the sea in whatever injured state the battle left it. When spearfishing, your prey has been personally selected as an invited guest of honor at your dinner table.

The day this story takes place found me snorkeling around in a little cove near Las Animas bay in the upper Sea of Cortez with speargun in hand, hunting for two medium-sized Cabrillo fish to bake in foil with salsa and onions for *Pescado en Papel* that evening. The first of the pair was already secured to the stringer on my weight belt as I submerged to survey some rocky structure to find another dinner companion.

There was a sudden tug upward on my belt that caught me completely by surprise, for I had begun this hunt as a solo venture. After surfacing, I found myself eye to eye with a very large pelican, and he seemed none too happy about sharing his private stock of fish with me.

"Arrgghhh!" I roared as a powerful kick from my three-foot-long swim fins propelled me up and out of the water to my waist. The pelican back-pedaled off about six feet but did not look at all like the frightened bird I'd expected to see, as I went back to my hunt.

Having spotted the rest of dinner, I was grabbing a few last breaths before diving to give chase while keeping my eye on my target. Another surprise stopped my breath when the pelican swam back and gripped the bright orange surface end of my snorkel and gave it a good tug. "This is a very determined pelican," I thought. Ways to mount a surprise counter attack came to mind. My weapons were my speargun and my knife, but I wanted no responsibility for wounding one of natures critters who I had no intention of eating.

A surprise submerged attack was planned, for I had superior command of the underwater portion of our impromptu battlefield. I could use the padded butt end of my gun as a medieval knight might use a padded lance for the first joust, knocking the wind from my opponent and perhaps driving him from the field. With a quick full breath I dove to the bottom and patiently held on to a large rock until the pelican had swum nearly overhead.

My target in my sights, I shot toward the surface holding my speargun firmly as it punched the pelican with what I thought would be a formidable blow that would drive the mighty bird to wing. Surprise again, for the pelican absorbed all the energy of my blow with little more notice than would the earth if you smote it with a tack hammer.

I'd read somewhere that when violence and intimidation fail, bribery can sometimes be an effective resort, so I offered the pelican my fish. The bribe was accepted and I returned to my hunt undisturbed, but the pelican stayed in the area until I had two new fish secured to my belt.

Later we enjoyed our dinner in the cockpit with the pelican paddling about nearby. He fixed me in his steady glare to remind me that our detente was only a temporary thing. It was obvious that from his point of view, he was sharing his fish with me, in spite of the fact that it was my hand he had eaten out of as he took my bribe.

The takeaway from this experience is the wisdom of: Take a little, leave a little, and balance will be found.

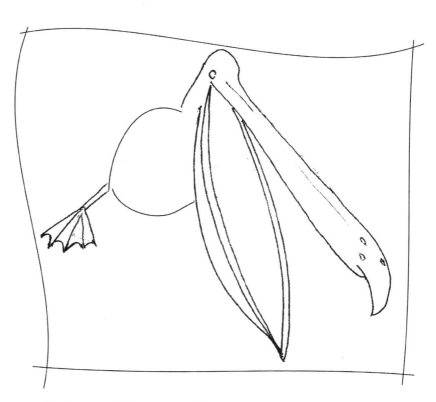

Underwater looking up at a hungry pelican diving for my fish

[2.05] *How Many Life Forms in This Square Meter?*

Sea of Cortez Race Week was a cruiser festival held each spring. Starting with a sailboat race from La Paz, the fleet rendezvoused at a large anchorage near Isla Partida about thirty miles to the north. Along with the racing there were many shoreside activities including beach volleyball, bikini contests, and lots of things for the cruising kids to do.

These cruising kids are a special lot with many skills not commonly found ashore. Most were exceedingly responsible, able to stand watch alone at night or power a high-speed dinghy a few miles to a favored dive spot. They also have special social skills, being capable of carrying on interesting conversations with a grown-up on a variety of subjects. The thing I found most amazing is how a gang of these kids could come together after the isolation of their family boat at sea, sorting themselves out immediately and beginning whatever game or opportunity for exploration was at hand.

The subject of this story is an activity created for the kids by one of the cruisers, a retired biology teacher, who carried the widest array of magnifying glasses and hand magnifiers I'd seen in one place. He also had a good supply of large nails and bright orange string, with which he marked out a patch of the scrubby desert shore adjacent to the beach in one meter squares.

Each kid was handed a magnifier, a pencil, and a pad of paper, then assigned a square to examine. The object of the activity was to find as many different life forms as possible within the assigned square, writing the name of any that could be identified and drawing a picture of each of the others for which the kid had no name. The time limit was supposed to be one hour and prizes were to be given for most entries by each of several age groups.

The surprise came when the hour's time had expired and none of the kids wanted to turn in their lists and sketches, even though some of the older kids had several pages of entries. They had little interest in winning the prizes from their participating in a contest. They were certain the rewards of the activity were greater than the prizes could be, so they continued their surveys, with some of the older kids helping the younger with names and other information.

The coda of this event for me was overhearing one pre-teen kid telling of the event to his grandmother on a phone patch over the ham radio.

"And Grammy, I found over a hundred different living things in that one small patch of what looked like nothing. Over."

Suited up to invite life forms for lunch—
Lycra swimming suit protects frtom sun and aquamales *(stinging jellyfish).*

[2.06]Communication Builds and Binds Communities

Radio communication was a central feature of life aboard a boat cruising Mexico during the '90s and served many important functions.

VHF radio generally has a short "line of sight" transmission range so it was the choice for local communication (within about a 25 mile radius if the antenna was mounted on a sailboat's masthead and less if the antenna was closer to the water). In populated anchorages it was the custom to leave your radio on during the day in the same way you would carry your cell phone so you could answer anyone calling you. Channel 22 was commonly used for this purpose, and, as no individual license was required, everyone could use these frequencies.

Privacy was largely eliminated in VHF communication, for a calling party's transmission would echo about the community on the multitude of monitoring radios. When the parties connect on channel 22 they would politely select another vacant channel they could switch to so their conversation would not be widely broadcast as was their meeting call. However any eavesdropper could follow the conversation to the new channel and be privy to all that was said.

Some would try to circumvent the followers by having agreed upon a "secret channel" that their intimate group would use, but that ruse was easily defeated with a quick spin of the dial to find the communicators' new channel. As anyone wishing to be available for general communication forfeited their privacy rights as soon as they turned on the radio, the community took on the character of a village with a single party line to handle all the residents. (Younger readers who are barely familiar with a land-line telephone will have to stretch their imaginations a bit to understand the concept of a party line.) Since most everyone knew what most everyone else was doing, these impromptu cruiser communities took on the character of a small town where some families went back a generation or two.

High Frequency radio was divided between the Ham radio frequencies and those of the "marine single-sideband", abbreviated as SSB, assigned channels. Only a ship's license was required for the marine SSB use so it was popular with those who didn't want to study and pass the examinations required for the various classes of Ham license which gave access to a much wider variety of frequencies than the SSB.

We just heard a fraction of a "phone patch" conversation between the youngster and his grandmother in the last story, so let that be the segue into the next chapter with some of my radio tales and customs.

3

RADIO COMMUNICATIONS

Ham radio was the primary communication media along the mexican coast in the early 1990s before land-based internet and cell phone coverage became ubiquitous. I had a buddy in junior high school who ran an amateur radio station with his father and I was a "SWL", a short wave listener, throughout my mid-teenage years. That was my foundation when I first sailed down the Pacific coast of Mexico and began my decade as Tech-Plus level Ham radio operator KC6-PXN.

[3.01] Racing Fun — The Melaque to Tenacatita Regatta

Here is some of the fun I had mixing a bit of racing into the sailing styles of the cruisers and their non-race boats. The setting this time is the mainland Pacific coast of Mexico within a day's sail north of Manzanillo, a busy port city and location of the famous Las Hadas Hotel. The sketch here shows the coast from Bahia (Spanish for bay) Tenacatita to Bahia Navidad.

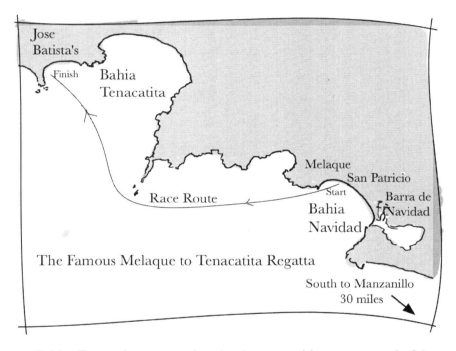

Bahia Tenacatita was a favorite layover with many wonderful features. There was a little anchorage just inside the north end, next to a shallow fish-filled rocky area we called "The Aquarium" because it was a favorite snorkeling spot. Bastista's was the last in a row of six similar small restaurants that functioned just fine in spite of not being connected to water, sewer, or electric grids. Indeed, Jose, Batista's owner, distrusted refrigeration because an un-noticed electrical failure could result in deadly bacteria growth. If the fish got warm because all the ice melted you knew it because the ice was gone, he reasoned. Clams and oysters were kept alive in net bags tied to an underwater rock formation about seventy-five feet from Batista's beach, where Jose would swim to restock the kitchen as needed.

For those readers unfamiliar with beach dining along the less developed mainland Pacific coast, a palapa restaurant consists of some tables and chairs planted in the beach sand under the shade of a palm frond roof. Informal to the extreme, it is not unusual to have a friendly dog snoozing under an adjacent table. A hammock or two usually hang in the shade where you might find a dozing grandfather with a small child asleep at his side.

Less than a hundred yards beyond the beach was a tidal lagoon that wound for a mile or more through the mangroves and emerged at the larger anchorage deep within the bay.

With an inflatable two-man kayak, the portage across the beach was easy and led directly to "the jungle tour" with its intimate exposure to a world of natural wonders. Utilizing proper tidal timing, the kayak would float silently, needing only an occasional paddle stroke to stay on course. In our quiet stealth mode we could drift down within feet of snoozing snowy egrets, watching them lazily awake and fly off with what seemed like only a couple strokes of their giant white wings.

Because most social communication between cruisers at anchor was on ch. 22 of the VHF radio, the party line made it easy to keep track of who was where. We could count on some friend for an invitation into a shaded cockpit with a cold beverage when we emerged into the inner bay while awaiting the tide to flood for the return trip up the jungle.

One great joy of that decade was the awareness that these days were indeed "The Good Old Days" and it was our responsibility to enjoy them. We also knew it was our responsibility to make our own fun. The "First Annual Melaque to Tenacatita Sailing Regatta" was one of those fun things we invented.

March 17 is St. Patrick's Day, and in Bahia Navidad south of Tenacatita lies the town of San Patricio where March 17 is the most celebrated holiday of the year. So celebrated that it takes a whole week to complete the events which include pre-dawn fireworks, late night beachfront music and dancing, and a host of daytime activities including a rodeo and a traveling circus.

The rodeo included such events as a game of polo in the dirt oval using a greased pig as the ball with the players riding horses not much taller than large-breed dogs.

In a tent not far from the rodeo ring was The Circus American with its theme proudly expressed in red, white, and blue sequined costumes. The opening act revealed a number of ramps, ladders, platforms, and other obstacles around the single ring. There was a large iron hoop as the last flaming portal for the troupe of full-sized pigs in their sequined capes to gallop through.

La Fiesta de San Patricio was a popular event with the cruising fleet working their way north in the spring to avoid the increasing heat and humidity of the mainland to the south where they had wintered. Bahia Navidad (Christmas Bay in English) with its trio of towns, Melaque to the north and beautiful Barra de Navidad to the south had plenty to keep the cruisers entertained for their stop-over.

March 19 happened to be Jose Batista's birthday and I had the good fortune to have been at two previous birthday parties Jose hosted for himself. Jose was so proud of the few yachts that would anchor in front of his restaurant and join his party that he kept a bound log book with attached photos, messages, and such to document their visits.

The confluence of all these factors gave me an idea and the Regatta was born. The race would have a "La Mans" start from the beach in front of Los Pelicanos restaurant in Melaque, with the skippers making their way from the beach to their boats at anchor. Anchors would be weighed and sails would be hoisted as the fleet exited the bay, starting their seventeen-mile race. The finish line would be on the beach at Batista's and time would be taken when the skipper anchored his vessel, made his way to shore, and presented his birthday gift to Jose. This ought to work, I thought, and I had a year to put forces in motion.

As the VHF radio provided "party line" style communication for cruisers within close range of one another, the Ham radio provided the long-range party line that connected most of the cruiser fleet in Mexico. The Ham radio would be my mouthpiece to promote this event, a promotion that began in earnest the following December.

Ham radio "nets" are daily on-air meetings of interested radio operators at specified times on specified ham radio frequencies. The Sonrisa Net was the first net in the morning, held on a shorter range frequency used mostly by the cruising boats in Mexico. The Chubasco and the Baja Nets followed with their many stateside operators providing news and "phone patch" communication from the boats to stateside family and friends.

Each net's format provided a segment for questions to be asked and answers provided—that is where I planted the seed.

"Has anyone heard anything about a sailing regatta in Melaque next year?" I asked.

"No, I haven't heard anything," was the answer from several respondents on the Chubasco Net that December morning.

A few days later I repeated the same question on the Baja Net, but this time one stateside ham replied he'd heard something about it on one of the other nets a few days ago. The seed had sprouted! The next step was my phone patch call to my mother a few days later.

Ham communication is simplex with radios capable of either transmission or receive modes, so you either talk or listen, saying "Over" when you have finished talking so the other party knows when they can speak. With a phone patch, this protocol is even more important because the stateside ham radio operator has to flip his switch with each "Over" to change the direction of communication from phone line to radio or from radio to phone line.

However the rest of the radios on that frequency can hear both sides of the conversation and there is much listening in because several different folks are awaiting their turn to phone home. And there were many who just listened in for some breakfast time entertainment and a chance to keep up on the latest gossip.

"Hi Mom, Over."

"Hi Tim. How are you doing and what's up with you? Over."

"All is fine and we're really enjoying those beer batter bread mixes you sent down. We are anchored here in Zihuatanejo. The next big event on our schedule is the Melaque to Tenacatita Regatta next March, Over"

"What's that? Over." So I proceeded to regale my mother with many wonderful details of a reality that existed only in my imagination.

A question about the regatta on the nets a few days later produced many of the details I had shared with my mother.

"I heard there were going to be prizes valuable beyond all belief," a friend in the know volunteered.

The magic was working.

I'll skip the many fun details and just tell you we managed to recruit seventeen competing boats with over sixty sailors who anchored one at a time in front of Jose's palapa. Jose beamed with pride as a delegation from each arriving boat boarded their dinghies and paddled ashore to present their gift.

The trophy presentation brunch the next morning yielded many memorable quotes. One cruiser who had been over served from the cask of mescal open to all declared:

"I woke up the next morning in clean underwear with no hangover. What was that stuff?"

Others expressed their satisfaction from knowing they can sail off their anchor, to a destination, and re-anchor under sail.

"I never thought about doing it until I did it, so now I know I can."

This regatta was rewarding on several levels beyond a bit of polish for sailing skills. Bonding a group of boats and sailors into a competition that was completely for the fun of it climaxed with the merger of the sailors and Jose's birthday party. Soon it was like we all had been family and neighbors for years.

Top Photo Shows Skippers Assembled for Le Mans *Start*
Bottom Photo Shows Skippers and Crew at Finish Line

[3.02] Well and Good

The Ham radio was the center of much social life during my decade in Mexico for it was the binder that kept the community in touch. There are are groups called "nets" who meet together on the same frequency on a regular schedule, and each net usually has a net controller or a set of controllers who rotate days so that no ship's batteries get too depleted.

I was the Saturday controller for the Sonrisa Net, *sonrisa* being the Spanish word for smile, and I tried to make those listening do just that. (For a nearly a decade strangers would come up to me with a warm hug or handshake, answering my surprised look with, "I know you've never met me but I've been having breakfast with you for the last year.")

The radio net was a place where you could get answers to vital questions of the moment. Subjects from first aid, to weather forecasts, to fishing reports, or how to get a balky diesel running right were just a few examples. But I got a new one from the wife of one of our regular members who was home schooling their kids.

"How can I get them to understand the difference between an adverb and an adjective?" she asked.

"Well & good", I replied. "I don't smell well - I don't smell good."

Later she regaled me with stories of the extreme edges of grossness the kids continued to explore while convincing their mom they understood how to use modifiers.

Tis the set of the sails,
not the strength of the gales
that determine the way we go.

Men in a ship are always looking up,
and men ashore are usually looking down

[3.03] Script Your Emergency for Effective Communication

Mastering a high level of seamanship is a primary goal for every yachtsman, and effective emergency radio communication is one vitally important seamanship skill. Visualizing communication like a movie is one useful path toward mastering the radio in an emergency.

Radio Rehearsal For Emergency Preparedness

Mentally rehearsing various scenarios is something all accomplished skippers do to help them prepare for various potential emergencies. Imagining a fire onboard while at sea sets the stage for mentally rehearsing how such fires could be fought.

Imagining an engine room fire leads to considerations like having an extinguisher (or two) within easy reach of the engine room access.

Mentally rehearsing opening the engine room door with flames leaping into your face leads to consideration of automatic engine room extinguishers and "fire fighting ports" that enable aiming an extinguisher into the engine room without opening the door.

The same mental-imaging principle applies to man overboard gear systems, first aid preparedness, EPIRBs, life rafts, and all the rest. Mentally rehearsing the various scenarios can help make for better preparation decisions, as well as producing better performance in actual emergency situations.

So here is where a screenwriter's skills come in to improve your mental rehearsals for emergency radio communications.

The above examples happen in a single scene or stage set, but imagine that we are on the boat dealing with fire, or man overboard (MOB), or injury, or potential sinking. Emergency radio communications involve two or more scenes. The boat in distress and the Coast Guard's radio room are two of the scenes the screenwriter would describe and populate with a cast of characters. Other rescue agencies, such as harbor patrol or Sea Rescue might also participate in this scenario, as might other recreational or commercial boats in the area.

The screenwriter visualizes each of these stage sets, considering which cast members are in each scene, what each of those actors knows, what they don't know, and what information they need in order to advance the story. The script could have the camera cut from the skipper with onboard radio to the Coast Guard radio room. There could be a split-screen image of another boat monitoring the emergency communications and making notes of the distressed boat's position, its visual description, nature of the emergency, and number of souls onboard.

Someone just listening in and taking notes could be a most valuable character should radio problems, like fire or electrical failure onboard the distressed vessel prevent additional communications to the rescue agency. Frequently a relay of vital information is required to properly inform the rescuers.

Imagine hearing the Coast Guard requesting a repeat transmission from the distressed vessel and hearing nothing but a garbled transmission from the skipper. How much better to have accurate information written down that can be quickly relayed?

Script Your Emergency

Now imagine you are the radio operator on the distressed vessel and you know that communicating your exact position is vital. Do you read this off the GPS every time you repeat your Lat/Lon numbers? If your boat is moving, will it be confusing for the last digit or two of the numbers to keep changing?

Unless you are speeding toward port, you are best not to update your exact position with each transmission for that generates too many different numbers.

Mentally rehearsing this part of the movie, where communications are repeated and checked and relayed as the camera cuts from shot to shot will convince you that writing some notes will help you repeat your speech accurately each time. Hearing with the mind's ear all these position numbers repeated two or three times might lead you to drop the last decimal place altogether, when reporting your position, being sure to declare in each transmission whether you are giving decimal minutes or minutes and seconds. (Be sure to know the difference!)

Imagine your reaction to Coast Guard requests as to how many PFDs and fire extinguishers you have onboard, things that seem like stupid distractions—for you are dealing with a crew member who just collapsed after being beaned by the spinnaker pole or gashed a femoral artery with the fishing gaff, or the cabin sole is awash with sea water. The screenwriter will see the pad in front of the Coast Guard radio man, and there is a blank for that information, along with lots of other stuff. If you write all the variations of that scene as you sarcastically reply to irritating questions, you see the best way to get through that section of the script and on to the important stuff is to be accurate and concise. The facts matter now. Your opinions don't.

A good mental rehearsal will stimulate your emotional reactions, which should also be noted so you'll be performance-ready should you have to step on stage and play the role. Be prepared for everything to be more difficult because of the stress you'll encounter when you perform in real emergency communication. Plan to do things like taking lots of notes and writing key information down clearly. Putting things in writing not only helps you to be consistently accurate, but also permits another radio operator onboard to step in if you have to leave the radio to attend to some other aspect of the emergency.

Some characters in this movie will require different information than others. If you are in a little patch of particularly nasty sea, the Coast Guard should be told while a nearby recreational boat would already be aware of this. If it is a medical emergency, detailed information about the nature of the problem and the present state of the victim will be quite valuable to medical people on frequency, but if there is no such expert listening, you are better to stick to more general descriptions.

When out of radio range of the primary rescue agency, you may have to rely on a relay from an inexperienced radio operator. Imagining this scene where you have a slightly intoxicated fisherman relaying detailed medical information might suggest how important it will be for you to organize your information so that it can be best communicated. Even communicating with the sharpest operator will go better if your information is well organized and prioritized.

And spend some time listening in on other radio communications when you are around your boat. Just as our screenwriter would be researching the crowd activity at a Dodgers game before writing such a scene for his movie, do some listening to put yourself in your emergency scene.

You will be entertained by operators who feel it is best to repeat each bit of information two or three times, but changing their syntax for each repetition so you're never certain whether it is a repetition or a correction. You will hear operators spelling out words using made up phonetic alphabets. This will be a fine reminder of the value of posting a "Radio Facts Card" (available at most boat stores) that lists things like proper frequencies to use and the universal phonetic alphabet.

So, imagine each of the situations and write your script so you can be an effective player when your movie runs.

Scallywag• US Doc. 267283• Call Sign WBP 8989 •37-foot Sailboat
Phonetic Alphabet

Alpha	Juliet	Sierra
Bravo	Kilowatt	Tango
Charlie	Lima	Uniform
Delta	Mike	Victor
Echo	November	Whiskey
Foxtrot	Oscar	X-Ray
Golf	Papa	Yankee
Hotel	Quebec	Zulu
India	Romeo	

[3.04] Weather Radio

Listening Carefully and Common Sense

When I began sailing offshore, radio listening was frequently the only source of weather information. It was NOAA weather broadcasts on high frequency radio and/or reports from Ham radio nets whose schedules set my schedules, for good weather information helps good decision making.

Listening to the NOAA broadcasts was most difficult and frustrating, especially at the beginning when I was uncertain of the broadcast format and when my area would be covered. If something was missed, there was no opportunity to rewind the broadcast until I purchased a micro cassette recorder just for that purpose.

There were frustrating sessions when I set the recorder near the radio speaker and some other task would intrude. Imagining the forecast had been captured on tape my attention was diverted to the new task, requiring searching the tape with crude forward and rewind controls that sometimes took you to an old forecast you did not realize was for last week. The recorder was soon banished to the bowels of the electrical locker.

Ham radio nets were more user-friendly after I became a regular participant. Opportunities to ask questions or to hear local reported conditions helped ensure good access to vital information, but communication still relied on the human ability to hear and to process information.

Once accustomed to listening carefully to the radio and taking notes to track important information as it was given, careful listening became a pleasant process of concentration, offering a relaxation similar to what you might get from concentrating on a puzzle of some sort. I discovered on the radio that one cannot listen while talking. Furthermore, without focused attention there is little retention

The surprise bonus of developing listening and information processing skills was their usefulness in social situations. I became a more valuable conversation partner as my radio skills developed.

[3.05] Radio Communication Techniques

Communicating on the radio is easy, just like talking on a cell phone, right? No. There are some important differences, and most of them are common sense things that are easy to keep in mind.

The first step in any communication is to establish contact, which is easy on a cell phone because the caller knows who is answering the call and the receiver checks the caller I.D to know who is on the other end. Radio communication requires a few more steps to establish contact because both parties need to identify themselves and also report to each other on the clarity of their transmissions. This information is important so that each party knows whether they must speak slowly and verify each step of the conversation as would be necessary if one station's signal was weak or if there was local radio interference reducing intelligibility for that station.

Most radio conversations take place on open radio channels, so other traffic on that frequency can interfere with communication, requiring both parties to agree on protocol for moving to another frequency. Likewise, it is possible for a new conversation to interfere with one in progress by other parties using the frequency. In the example of radio nets, there can be a group discussion between stations that are so widely spread that most of the stations are out of range of your reciever leading you to think the channel or frequency is clear. For this reason a transmission should begin with the query, "Is this frequency in use?" along with the identification of the transmitting station like "This is Kilo Charlie 6 Papa X-Ray November."

If there happen to be one or more stations participating in the established net or conversation who are within range of your transmission, having your identity enables them to respond directly to you so you know to move to a different frequency.

Sometimes your transmission involves something of an emergency nature or an overriding need to complete *time value traffic*, which is communication that needs to be complete before some time deadline. By declaring a priority nature, other stations on frequency permit you to break in with your message or concern, mustering the resources of all the folks hearing you. It is then your obligation to clearly identify yourself, your location, and the nature of your traffic.

To avoid getting lost in stage fright or otherwise getting tongue-tied or just rambling on, organize your thoughts first, making notes if needed, to list your main points of information and the order of their presentation. A small notebook kept close to the radios is most useful.

A small group of Ham radio operators I knew in Mexico awarded a prize—"The Largest Speech for the Smallest Thought"—not a prize to covet.

Until you become a comfortable and experienced radio operator, make a habit of being well organized and clear spoken.

[3.06] Ham 'n Bees

My first month cruising on *Scallywag*, a 1974 vintage Islander 37-foot sloop, brought me many valuable lessons, one of which was the usefulness of radio communication as a balancing factor to counterweigh the disconnection experienced while living off the grid in remote locales.

As previously stated, many ham radio operators organize themselves into networks and meet together on a prearranged frequency at a prearranged time. The maritime nets provided essential weather information, along with a cornucopia of other benefits to the cruising sailor, giving any licensed radio operator immediate access to a wealth of resources.

About forty-five miles north of Puerto Vallarta there is a wide and shallow bay named Jaltemba, with a sand beach that stretches six miles. It was there we decided to hang out for a few days to relax and resupply beer and tortillas.

Anchored in a bit of shelter behind the only island in the bay we were well off shore and away from the insect populations that could be intense along the jungled mainland. We were adjacent the local tourist snorkeling rocks, so there was plenty to see.

The next afternoon we returned from our shoreside resupply excursion and saw a few bees buzzing about the cockpit, which were a concern because of my allergy to their sting. My first move was to go below to retrieve my anna-kit syringe, jacket, and gloves. I emerged to find the bee population had greatly increased in the cockpit.

We retreated below and screened and sealed the cabin as we had done in San Blas against the no-see-ums, and considered how to react to this insect siege.

Although still a new operator, I had listened in to Ham nets enough to know that there was always somebody who has some little known fact whenever it was required. I turned on the radio and started scanning the 40 meter band to see if I could find any late afternoon stateside nets, and was soon rewarded to hear an operator identify Salome, Arizona, as his QTH, or location.

"Break, Break." I broadcast and listened for a response.

"I heard a breaker in there folks," announced the net controller. "Listen up everyone. Go ahead breaker."

I identified myself, stated my location, and then explained I needed to know what to do about a sudden bee infestation.

"Anyone on frequency know anything about bees?" asked the net controller and there ensued some relay work and then someone making a land line "two-ringer" to bring a Colorado bee-keeper friend named Fred on frequency to hear the nature of our difficulty. (A "Two Ringer" is a commonly used signal one land-line phone can make to another, avoiding a long distance toll charge for the connection that was never completed.)

Fred announced his call sign, signaling his arrival on frequency within a few minutes. Another land-based station explained the nature of our dilemma, omitting only the information that we were on a sailboat anchored off the coast of Mexico.

"These bees won't hurt you at all" was a most comforting thing to hear as Fred began explaining bee behavior.

"The colony is traveling to a new location and have no energy to waste in attacking you. They gorged themselves as much as they could to fuel up for their journey so they are too bloated to mount an effective attack even if they wanted to. Pretty soon the queen will settle in and all the bees will clump around her in a big ball to sleep and rest up for tomorrow." Fred went on to explain.

A short venture topsides in protective clothing found the bees had indeed formed a basketball-sized cluster on the underside of the canvas cockpit dodger. I reported the news to Fred.

"No problem now." he said. "Just get a big cardboard box and hold it under the mass of bees. Give the awning (the boat's dodger had been transformed into an awning somehow in the relay process) a big thump and the cluster will fall into the box. Then just close it up and walk it into the woods."

As soon as I could control my laughter, I explained our sailboat was anchored offshore and we did not have a large cardboard box in our inventory of emergency supplies. Even if we had such a box, insurmountable obstacles remained to our walking into the non-existent woods after sharing a small dinghy with a bunch of buzzing bees.

I asked for an alternative plan.

"Well, then just relax and hang out down below for a little longer and they'll all be sound asleep. Go about your business and they'll all leave at sunrise." Fred advised.

We did. They did. And all the evidence that remained the next morning were a few dead bees and a few more dying ones fluttering about on the cockpit sole.

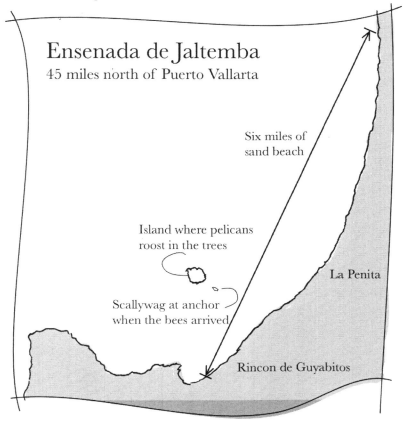

Ensenada de Jaltemba
45 miles north of Puerto Vallarta

Six miles of
sand beach

Island where pelicans
roost in the trees

La Penita

Scallywag at anchor
when the bees arrived

Rincon de Guyabitos

4

CRUISING LESSONS

[4.01] Mind Over Temperature

Attitude and expectation have tremendous influence over our level of satisfaction and one fine Canadian couple expressed this marvelously with a custom they practiced religiously on their cruising boat *Telethia*.

Summer in the Sea of Cortez is both a wonderful and a trying experience. Very hot weather is the norm and high humidity conditions occur when hurricane weather patterns develop. Lots of shade, little clothing, and as much time in the water as possible were the main defenses.

The first ham net in the morning for the Mexico cruisers was the Sonrisa (or Smile) net where boats would check in from various areas with their local weather report, which always included the temperature. Each morning John & Laura would report a temperature on their *Telitha* that was ten to twenty degrees below any boat in their general area. They never complained about the heat.

Now I knew of a wonderful little anchorage at Isla Smith near Bahia Los Angeles that had a built-in "air conditioner." There is a volcanic cone that rises about 1500 feet above the anchorage, and the prevailing winds blow from that direction. Airplane pilots and physicists will explain how air temperature drops with elevation as it moves up this cone and cools some more with its expansion as it spreads down the hill.

I thought perhaps *Telitha* had several such magic spots where they spent their time.

It was a different magic they conjured, for instead of a thermometer on board, *Telitha* had a small blackboard on which they'd chalk a number.

Attitude adjustment for cruising contentment

[4.02] Use What You Know to Address the Unknown

Don't be intimidated by what you don't know. Start working with what you do know. Use the bit you do know as the starting point and keep an open mind as you recognize and select alternatives.

One reason sailors go to sea is to encounter the unknown, whether it be the customs at a foreign port of call, the first experience in heavy weather, or even the inevitable breakdowns that occur with annoying regularity. I was given a valuable lesson about such encounters while listening to a retired high school automobile shop teacher address a group of cruising skippers in Mazatlan. That group of skippers were from backgrounds ranging from doctor, lawyer, teacher, and fireman. None were engine mechanics.

"Sure you will feel lost the first time your diesel engine doesn't run because you feel you know nothing about the subject. My message is that you know *something* about *most things*, and if you focus on what you know, you will be on your way finding the answers you need—while focusing on what you don't know will paralyze you into inaction."

"In the case of your diesel engine, you know you need battery power to turn the motor over when you turn the key. If the motor turns over you know the electrical side of things is functioning and you look elsewhere. If it doesn't turn over, you're on track to finding the problem as you check first the battery power and then the switches and starter wiring."

He went on to list the basic facts the skippers did know and demonstrated in his discussion how the same technique could be followed in determining if fuel was reaching the cylinders, and tracing problems through bleeding air from the system to checking filters, and through the list of reasonable and logical steps that even an uninformed skipper could take to solve his problem.

"Not too big a jump from dealing with the unknowns of diesel failure to dealing with other problems." thought I.

We all do know something about most of the things a sailor can encounter so it is wise of us to hone our skills at leveraging what we know to help us find our way through the new frontiers we encounter.

[4.03] Save your Hide with Cockpit Spray

Life aboard a sailboat is idyllic but exposed skin takes a beating—and most skin is exposed during the hot summers of Baja California. Between the effects of the sun, the drying action of frequent saltwater immersion, and the occasional insect attack my thin Irish flesh felt under constant assault until Avon's Skin So Soft came to my rescue.

This bath oil product has some miraculous insect-repelling power without the objectionable irritation and smell of other repellants. When dispensed from a spray-cleaner type bottle, after-shower skin could be misted with a cooling spray while providing a slick moist base on which to spread sunscreen.

Scallywag had a T-shaped cockpit with the aft portion divided off by the steering wheel and a bulkhead to the height of the cockpit seats. This back area was both the shower and the "mud room" where sandy feet would be washed after returning from the dinghy. With a handy sarong clothes-pinned to the wheel and lifelines, a modest person could maintain privacy while seated.

A small plastic box held the Skin So Soft spray bottle with its contents of the highly diluted bath oil; along with the ear wash mixture in its squeeze bottle, the sunscreen, the soap, shampoo, and the hair conditioner. With all handy next to the freshwater shower spray, and pressure seawater sprayer used during fish cleaning and other heavy use applications—simple comforts abounded.

[4.04] Here's to Ear Health

I spent much of my youth around swimming pools where many were victims of "swimmer's ear." When I spent my first summer in the Sea of Cortez, swimmer's ear was also a common malady until I spread the word about my mother's prophylactic measures.

The warm water of this fertile gulf is a virtual biological soup of numerous tiny sea plants and animals that thrive in the warm moist incubator of a swimmer's ear. These are the agents that increase their population until they become an infection.

To thwart their growth, my mother would first instruct us to get as much water as possible out of our ears, and then she would rinse our ear canals with a 50/50 mixture of alcohol and vinegar dispensed from an eye dropper. The alcohol provided some disinfectant action, killing some of the plants and critters while it also provided some drying effect, removing water as it evaporated. The vinegar, good old acetic acid, changes the pH of the ear canal incubator which also disrupts the growth of most infectious agents.

I was always entertained when I'd pick up the bouquet of a fellow cruiser walking in town. We were the only ones who smelled of salad and Skin So Soft.

Don't put anything in your ear smaller than your elbow.

[4.05] The Sun is Not Your Friend

The long term effects of the sun's rays are hazardous. You should do your best to protect yourself and your guests from its harmful effects. These cumulative effects can add up to make many skin problems later in life. Many studies demonstrate the increased hazards of overexposure in youth, which can lead to serious and sometimes fatal results.

I am a fair-skinned blue-eyed Irishman who was a "water-rat" since well before I became a certified scuba diver at age 13 in 1958. I was the kid on the beach with a hat, a T-shirt, and white zinc oxide over any remaining exposed skin. I still got some painful burns. Lots of sailors I know were water rats who did not take such counter-measures as kids, and many of them are now dealing with various kinds of skin cancers—many more serious than the dozen or so spots that I have frozen away twice a year.

During my decade in Mexico, La Paz was a regular port of call where there was a dermatologist of great renown. At my first appointment, I was taken aback to discover that not only was she a woman doctor (still uncommon in Mexico at that time) but that she wanted me to strip 100% naked and stand on a short sturdy stool, for that was her examination procedure. After I complied, she spent the next fifteen minutes with a magnifying glass moving around the stool examining every square millimeter of my epidermis for trouble spots, much of which wore a bright red blush.

Sometimes there is no room for modesty.
Grin and bare it seemed the only course of action.

Although she had no English, she effectively communicated "El Sol's" danger—*muy peligroso!*—as she delivered my first taste of liquid nitrogen. Returning for near semiannual visits as instructed, I blushed less as I got used to the routine, although I never conquered my modesty enough to pursue a career in table dancing.

[4.06] Santa Ana Wind Schools a Sailor

Preparations for a prolonged cruise in Mexico on my 37-foot sloop *Scallywag* had been all consuming for many months, so we decided to decompress at Catalina Island after leaving the Pacific Mariner's Yacht Club guest dock in December twenty years ago. A cold NE wind was starting to build, so we anchored in the mouth of Cat Harbor on the protected lee side of the island about fifty yards upwind from a boat that looked familiar from my previous voyages South of the Border. A radio hail from my old friend Gil brought out future plans, fond memories of Mexico, and a dinner invitation.

The wind built as we dined, drank, and talked until it became obvious that we should start our short row home. Glowing from our fine evening but chilled by the powerful headwind, I rowed our recently procured 8-foot Del Rey Dinghy with its undersized oars away from the protection of our host's vessel, only to realize we were on the wrong side of an asymmetrical battle. Five minutes of stroking with all I had brought us no closer to *Scallywag* and we were crabbing away from our host boat as we slid backward toward the harbor entrance and the open sea.

Fortunately Gil had been monitoring our efforts and launched his powerful tender to collect us and render a most welcome tow home. How jolly it was to be sailing toward Mexico the next day instead of toward Hawaii that night.

Any fool can carry on, but a wise man knows how to shorten sail in time

5

THE SELF-SUFFICIENT SAILOR

[5.01] Rehearsing Priorities

This is a story about sailing from Puerto Vallarta, Mexico, north and across the Sea of Cortez to La Paz, with an unscheduled stop in Mazatlan to replace *Scallywag's* backstay after it suddenly broke.

It happened with a loud bang shortly after I tucked in the second reef at sunset as we beat into a stiff breeze and a nasty square chop. I had just reset the autopilot to steer about five degrees more off the wind to give us a bit more power and ease our ride.

The backstay parted just above the bottom turnbuckle, a surprising location considering it was just at the handy hold height from the comfortable "back porch" stern bench. That portion of the backstay was seen closely many times a day. It seems such failures are usually in rarely inspected locations because early signs are not seen. My only warning was an unfamiliar cracking sound that foreshadowed the exploding wire a minute or so before it blew.

My pick-up crewman was a fine Mexican lad in his early thirties named Armando. Though inexperienced in sailing and boating in general, he was a genial fellow and a quick learner. His English was better than my Spanish but he was always patiently willing to help my Spanish through various discussions about sailing and life in general. We were having a good time together as we thought about preparing our meal on this second night of our voyage.

KA-BOOM, it went and there was no doubt in my mind what it was as it shot past my ear. Fortunately the solar panel array through which the backstay passed, effectively diverted the whiplash of the parted wire from my vulnerable head.

"How might I help?" asked Armando as I set about the task of jury-rigging the deck-stepped mast to keep it upright in the boat.

"Down into the companionway!" I ordered, explaining I didn't want him to get injured and it would be easier for me to scurry about without someone in my way on the small sloop.

"Sometimes he who does nothing helps most." Armando declared with a warming smile as he ducked below.

It was important to prioritize what must be done and act quickly. Without the backstay, the leach of the mainsail was the only connection to the top part of the mast that was still opposing the pull of the headstay, which was now sagging badly as the masthead bent forward.

"What's keeping tension in that leach?" was the question that popped to mind.

"The mainsheet to the boom, the boom to the reefing line, and the reefing line to the sail — it's just that one slender reefing line keeping the rig in the boat!' I thought as I grabbed a handy piece of Spectra line and whipped several lashings to secure the reefing clew to the boom, eliminating the reefing line as the weak link.

Next, I tried in vain to roll up some of the jib to reduce the load on the mast but it proved impossible with the deeply sagging headstay. When bowed, the head stay sag reduces the power ratio of the furling drum. Normally, the drum's large diameter compared to the smaller diameter of the luff extrusion provides a mechanical advantage, easing the task of furling the sail. However, the bend of the sagging headstay reverses that advantage to a degree that furling is impossible. Having failed at furling the sail I sheeted the flapping jib more tightly to help stabilize the mast which was jumping about like a reed in the wind.

When the building wind waves get in phase with chop, the boat would move violently, waving its mast in enthusiasm. I grabbed both ends of the starboard spinnaker halyard, securing one end to a sturdy stern cleat and the other to the available starboard primary winch. This arrangement supplied considerable power and the headstay sag was somewhat less now, but I still couldn't budge the furling line.

I considered dropping the jib but decided I'd need it to provide some stability until I could secure effective backstay tension. Like the tightrope walker's fan, the steady force of the air against the sail's surface resisted the oscillations of the mast.

The port spinnaker halyard was then pressed into similar service, but secured to the smaller secondary winch as the primary port winch was serving the jib sheet—less than ideal but it could still add substantially to the support the other halyard was supplying.

"What next?" I thought. I had a four part "handy billy" vang tackle set-up that I used for lifting the 15 hp outboard to and from the dinghy, so it went in service with one end secured to the mainsail reef clew and the other to the sturdy stern cleat. I then re-tensioned the two spin halyards with their cockpit winches, and then went forward to pick up the running backstays and bring them aft to stabilize the mast a bit more.

There was still too much sag in the bowed headstay to roll up the jib, but the wind had abated somewhat and we were footing rather comfortably up the coast toward Mazatlan.

"Do you think we should have a cold beer now that our situation seems less perilous?" I yelled toward the companionway. Up came Armando's cheery face.

"I think we should postpone it until immediately!" he declared as he opened two cold Pacifico beers.

By ten o'clock that evening the wind had dropped to less than five knots and it was time to fire up the engine and finally roll up most of the jib so we could motor-sail the 25 or so miles up to Mazatlan's outer harbor. It was dead calm by the time we got anchored in the glassy harbor and celebrated with a last Pacifico after the main was stowed and covered. Soon we were dead asleep, relieved to be secure at last.

The story went on after we motored the few miles north at first light toward Marina Mazatlan where there were plenty of slips available. This turned out to be a wise decision because my spare length of standing rigging (I also had a good set of Sta-loc fittings to replace any wire needing it) turned out to be defective. After I had cut it to length and was fitting the second terminal, severe damage to the inner central bundle was revealed. I checked the other end and its core too was badly scraped and cut up as if the manufacturing die was badly damaged (but the manufacturer continued turning out the product none the less).

With several other cruisers in the harbor it took only a few minutes to locate another spare piece of wire and to arrange for its replacement in three weeks when another helpful cruiser would be returning from a doctor visit stateside.

Proving once again that it is indeed a small world, it turned out that three years previously, West Marine had a batch of bad wire from one of their offshore suppliers and my generous lender had bought his wire from the same defective batch as I had.

We fell back on plan B when no other unused wire was available and gained access to a large pile of rusty coils discarded by others, eventually sorting out a couple of lengths that had no visible surface damage.

Cutting into the first revealed a rotten core but the second piece was deemed serviceable. It was quickly put to work, and we set sail for a pleasant voyage to La Paz.

On my next trip stateside, I bought a sturdy length of Spectra and some eyebolt turnbuckle ends for the boat's emergency rigging kit.

Are there lessons here? U-betcha, there's loads.

1. Mental rehearsal for emergency situations is of utmost value. It is so much easier to accurately observe a familiar situation—something you've thought about before. Effectively analyzing an emergency and prioritizing your remedial actions will greatly improve your chances of success. I've had plenty of time to think about such things during my many days spent sailing about as a solo sailor. Imagining different scenarios and determining my course of action was an entertaining and educational game.

2. Seek out racing experiences with talented crew. You will see that well-prepared folks with a reasonable supply of gear and parts can successfully deal with emergencies. Experiencing such events will build your confidence. As you imagine emergency scenarios, maintain your confidence as you sort through the factors and alternatives that exist. The more you can do this sort of mental rehearsing, the greater your reserve of confidence and ingenuity will be.

3. A "Plan B" can be a perfectly acceptable solution so try to keep your mind open to alternatives. However, beware the trap of inventing too many alternatives. "One way to justify doing nothing is to continually suggest doing something else."

4. Stainless steel standing rigging deteriorates in ways that cannot easily be detected. Warm weather cruising far from the dockside freshwater wash and polish accelerate the wire rot, so realize the increased hazard of not refreshing your rig until well after its "sell by" date has expired. Ten years used to be considered a reasonable "working life" for standing rigging but eight might be a better age for the sailor who wants to be truly safe. A falling rig or an exploding stay can do great damage to boat and crew!

5. Be your own hero. Picture heroic action and picture yourself as that heroic actor. Prepare yourself for that role so if you get cast in the part, you'll be ready to perform.

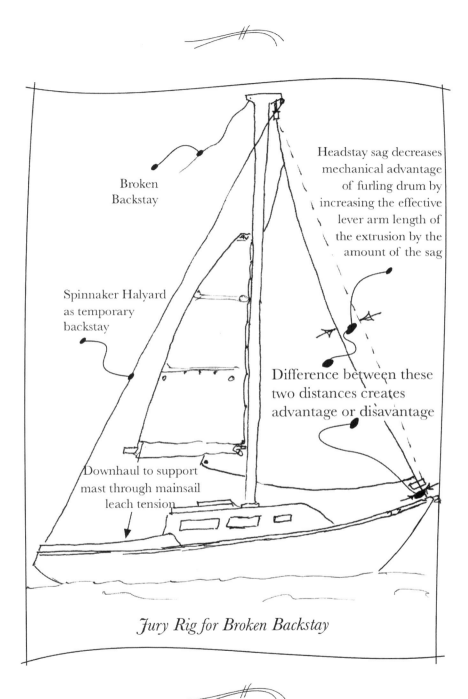

Broken
Backstay

Headstay sag decreases
mechanical advantage
of furling drum by
increasing the effective
lever arm length of
the extrusion by the
amount of the sag

Spinnaker Halyard
as temporary
backstay

Difference between these
two distances creates
advantage or disavantage

Downhaul to support
mast through mainsail
leach tension

Jury Rig for Broken Backstay

Mast Straightening in a Guerrilla Boatyard

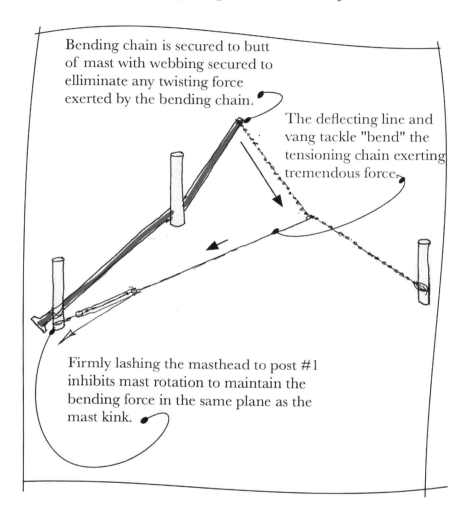

Bending chain is secured to butt of mast with webbing secured to elliminate any twisting force exerted by the bending chain.

The deflecting line and vang tackle "bend" the tensioning chain exerting tremendous force.

Firmly lashing the masthead to post #1 inhibits mast rotation to maintain the bending force in the same plane as the mast kink.

Taking your time to do a project is sometimes the only way to do it.

[5.02]"Poco a Poco"—A cruising lesson from Mexico

Self-sufficiency is tremendously rewarding and empowering. Confidence in your ability to manage most any situation comes from your previous successes. Embracing opportunities to face new challenges is one pathway to becoming a confident sailor. Here is a story about one such opportunity.

Puerto Escondido on the Baja Peninsula had a large dusty parking lot adjacent to the decaying small boat launching ramp. That lot became our *ad hoc* boatyard. Our project was to unstep the bent mast from a Yorktown 35, straighten and restep it. The Yorktown's skipper planned to sail south to La Paz where there is an abundance of skilled metal workers to perform a more permanent repair by cutting the mast and installing an internal stiffening sleeve, but he could not sail there without an immediate repair.

Unstepping and restepping masts are easy tasks I practiced during my racing days on my beloved Ranger 26, which involved dropping and redoing things on the mast several times.

With cooperating sailboats on each side, and coordinated handling of halyards on the adjoining boats, this process is quite simple. With a free halyard from each of the adjacent boats attached to a loop around the mast to be removed, coordinated tensioning of the two halyards pulls the loop up the mast until it reaches the mast's spreaders. A bit more cranking and the mast is lifted from its step and swung into a horizontal position to be lowered onto the deck. We had no difficulties transferring the stick onto a pair of dinghies, and ferrying it to the boat ramp.

For our bending apparatus, we were fortunate enough to have three sturdy posts arranged as shown.

I had learned in high school physics the tremendous mechanical advantage exerted by deflecting a tensioned chain or cable—the longer the length of cable, the more the deflecting force increases the tension. Sighting up a sailboat mast while pulling sideways on a shroud demonstrates these vectors with observable mast bend.

Our biggest problem was keeping all the volunteers from helping, We already had enough volunteers to reverse the bent mast into a crumpled hairpin. Directing the helpers away, I tensioned the vang tackle until the first signs of bending could be detected.

I went to the bend point with a light hammer, and began to tap the soft aluminum hard enough to make some noise but not so hard as to dent it. A friend who did crash repair on sports cars advised: "Bang it about a bit, and things [at the molecular level] will move around enough to relax the bend."

As I was returning to the vang tackle to tension it up a bit more, a nearby worker with a welding torch was setting up to heat up the bend. His point, as best as I could understand from his Baja accented spanish, was that we shouldn't mickey mouse around, but just heat it up and bend it straight.

"No! Por favor, poco a poco!"—poco a poco, a little bit at a time, was the best I could come up with, feeling my Spanish and his high school physics were both inadequate for an explanation of aluminum metallurgy. And that is how we straightened the bent mast—a bit more bending force and a bit more hammering on the deformed kink—a little bit at a time.

Now "Poco a Poco" is a valuable mechanical process for the competent mariner to fully understand.

Take my friend who was delivering a sedentary cruising ketch from Los Angeles to Hawaii. She was able to post updates about the trip with a satellite phone so it was easy to follow their story. They had just suffered their second spinnaker halyard chafing problem with their port spinnaker halyard—the morning after they completed spinnaker and dousing sock repairs necessitated by the starboard halyard's chafe failure.

"Poco a poco" some sharp edge aloft was sawing through their halyards, greatly accelerating the normal chafing wear the halyard suffers as the line stretches and recovers and as the sail oscillates about. Many offshore sailors learn that the joy of making a long passage frequently permits leaving sails without adjustment for extended periods. But the experienced sailor will periodically readjust all running rigging just a bit to spread the wear damage.

Anywhere that sails touch rigging should also be scrutinized for chafe. Remember seeing "baggy wrinkle," soft padding on traditional rope rigged boat spars & shrouds, which was utilized to reduce chafe on the linen sails of the times? Although baggy wrinkle has no place on a modern sailboat, the prudent sailor will do his best to smooth any surface the sail can contact.

A rigger friend of mine converted me from cotter pins to tiny machine bolts with Nyloc nuts to secure turnbuckles. With no sharp ends of cotter pins to worry about there was no need to tape turnbuckles which deprives the metal of the air it needs to remain corrosion resistant. Even if the rig stays perfectly in tune, it is still a good practice to lubricate and readjust the turnbuckles annually just to ensure they don't freeze up.

"Poco a poco," the natural movement of the boat can create chafe in many places besides sails and rigging. Engine hoses are a prime target, where vibration and sea motion can combine, little by little, turning a hose support bracket into an effective saw.

Extracting an anchor fouled in bottom growth (Please don't anchor in kelp for many reasons!) can seem impossibly difficult, but just snubbing the rode and letting the boat bob on the swells produces very effective lifting power, a little bit at a time. Get comfortable, re-snub the rode from time to time to take up the slack, and eventually it will work loose.

As a racer in remission, I'd frequently find myself sailing with non-racers who didn't quite understand how minor adjustments can have profound impact on sailing efficiency. "A little bit at a time," I'd urge, but still the genoa would go out a foot or be ground into the spreaders.

"Poco a poco" has become a catch phrase in much that I do, for it reminds me to observe the impact of my actions as adjustments are made.

Planning adjustments includes adjusting plans. Without that flexibility we are merely following a track rather than exploring options to find what is best.

Cruisers dinghy raft-up in Zihuatanejo
Rounding up a bunch of cruisers in sunny Mexican Ports is easy.

[5.03] Make Your Engine Room a Friendly Place to Visit

Scallywag's Engine Room - 21 hp 1981 Universal diesel

Many lessons come at a price. My tuition mushroomed exponentially when I was motor sailing in a light morning offshore breeze south out of Banderas Bay twenty three years ago, single handing toward Zihuatanejo. Returning to the cockpit with a fresh cup of coffee, I was alarmed to hear the engine oil pressure signal buzzing away and dove for the shut down control. As it turned out I was too late! The ancient hose that went from the engine block to the oil pressure sender, a hose that was well hidden under the exhaust manifold, had failed, spraying much of the 21 hp diesel's oil supply around the engine room. Lack of lubrication destroyed the oil pump and scored the pistons in the short time it took for me to hear the alarm and shut things down.

I turned 180 degrees, rolled out the jib, and began sailing toward Neuvo Vallarta, a marina where I knew I could find a slip and sail into it with my now engineless 37-foot sloop. And thus began my transition from a regular racing sailor who occasionally glanced with distain at the rusting mass in the bowels of the boat that usually ran only to get out to the starting line. I became a cruising sailor with a most intimate relationship to the power plant that supplied water and electricity in addition to propulsion.

After much adventure pulling the engine out of the boat, getting it into the Jeep supplied as my reward for attending a time share presentation, off to the machine shop, and back into the boat three weeks later, my diesel relationship was on an intimate new basis. I had learned to understand her needs, value her contribution, and monitor her welfare as never before—kind of like marriage.

One addition I made was a set of duplicate controls just inside the engine room door, which permitted me to look inside and check things out before I fired up my beloved companion to make sure all was well with her. As the compression release was close at hand, I could give her a few free revolutions to distribute her lubricating fluids before firing her off and watch her run for a bit to make sure belts, pumps, and hoses all were in good order. This was my standard starting procedure except in the rare cases where I had to remain at the helm.

A few years later this procedure enabled me to spot a failing motor mount before any damage occurred. The knowledge and confidence I gained from the previous engine removal and installation permitted me to install a new mount and realign the engine while anchored in the pleasant bay of Ensenada Grande. A few years after that the transmission self-destructed while motor sailing from San Carlos toward Puerta Vallarta. As the winds were light and nearly dead aft, I changed course to La Paz so I could beam reach under spinnaker and eventually sail into a Marina de La Paz slip directly in front of the Dock Restaurant windows.

With my newly acquired skills I was now well equipped to once again yank out the little diesel and wheel it up the dock ramp, however this time there was a much larger audience. As a well known voice on the radio networks, I felt obligated to share my situation and then to proudly proclaim that I could pull my engine off its mounts and get it onto the dock in less than an hour if one good soul would volunteer to help me. My old friend Mort, the restaurant's owner, saw an opportunity to get some extra business and offered to sell half price beers from an hour after I started work until the engine was on the dock cart.

Many volunteer helpers presented themselves, each with a few suggestions about how the job could be accomplished most efficiently— all of whom were thanked for their offers but rejected in favor of a large fireman down visiting his parents. He was strong, intelligent, open minded, and had no suggestions whatsoever—the perfect helper!

The next morning, Mort had a large bunch of beer drinkers watching disappointedly as the stopwatch read less than 45 minutes when the boom swung over and we lowered the now familiar little power plant into the cart.

Now, I am not suggesting that you need to field strip your engine and perform heroic repairs under iffy conditions, but I am suggesting that you do get more closely acquainted. Buy an hour or two from one of the area's accomplished marine engine mechanics and have him (or her) take you through oil and filter changes, bleeding the fuel system, checking pump impellers, squeezing hoses, and all the basic sensible periodic checks.

This is a good time to put your spare raw water impeller in service and save what you replaced for an emergency spare—a practice that insures you have both a spare that fits and that you have the knowledge and tools to replace it yourself. You may find a time when you must rely on yourself, and you might find this newfound friendship will save you from some serious problem in the future.

And even if you never have to use these newfound maintenance and repair skills, you will at least enjoy your life a bit more having the confidence you know your engine room better now.

Engine re-install team at Marina de La Paz, Mx.

Marina de La Paz Dock Restaurant and Observation Gallery

[5.04] Marine Professionals

You can observe a lot just by watching.

Every harbor has a community of professional boat workers with specialized skills ranging from sailmaking to marine electronics, from paint finishes to sailboat rigging, from engine mechanics to marine plumbing (nothing spoils a trip like plumbing problems), and almost every other skill required to keep a vessel in proper working order. There is a secondary community of folks who work on boats, most of whom don't have the highest level of professional skills but who can still deliver effective labor on repairs and upgrades. There are other levels, but you should be very selective about letting uninformed workers around expensive gear for your final costs can easily eclipse your anticipated savings.

I want to talk about the true professionals and their great value to us sailors (and power boaters too!).

Nearly every single bit of the boat represents one design decision out of many choices, and there are alternate paths to most repairs and upgrades. The true professional knows his craft well from the combination of years of experience usually following a period of apprenticeship where trial and error learning was more acceptable. This professional has chosen his (or her, of course) area of expertise because it was of compelling interest, and this is a continuing interest that drives their curiosity to ferret out new things while they remain curious about traditional solutions and how they have developed as an essential part of the craft.

It is nigh impossible for the part time sailor to access the data to select the best alternative course, and this is one area where the services of the true professional have enduring value. These professionals see many different applications and are educated enough that they can recognize success or failure of the original choice. Where a failure was the choice's result, the professional can assess the effectiveness of the various layers of repairs. These experiences provide an education available in no other manner.

Now consider that the best of these professionals enjoy being in a community where experiences are exchanged and useful sources of information are shared, providing a level of excellence comparable to the highest levels of academia. A wise sailor will recognize and utilize this aspect of the professionals to enlarge his body of knowledge. Most of these professionals will share priceless information and techniques in the course of working or consulting for you, so be a curious and attentive employer, and make a point of being around as the job is assessed and parts are ordered.

I am more curious about these things than most, but I am certain that any level of thoughtful curiosity will be generously rewarded. To witness and to understand the problem solving-techniques of professionals will enlighten many unrelated pursuits to come. Skill and confidence in problem solving are better than money in the bank!

One last word—this community of professionals can only survive if they have a critical mass of employers appreciating their work. Asking owners and managers of boats similar to yours can steer you to the higher levels of this community—and because it is a community, a professional in one area can frequently refer you to one in another area. These professionals are occasionally the lowest bidder, but even when their fee is significantly higher it is usually the best value for a job of complexity and importance.

Even if your personal budget ensures this will be a do-it-yourself job, buying an hour or two from a consultant to put you on the right path will be the small investment you'll remember as you look upon this project or system in the future—satisfied that you made good decisions.

[5.05] Physics and Philosophy

I am frequently enlightened while meandering around the intersection of physics and philosophy. This particular meander started during a Groupon special introductory airplane flight out of Santa Monica Airport that Debby had purchased months ago. We had saved it for a wedding anniversary present to ourselves, and found a beautiful So Cal day to cash it in.

And cash in we did! I sat in the pilot's left seat, with noble instructor Terrence in the co-pilot's to my right. After extensive pre-flight checking and various safety procedures explained, we taxied and took off.

Heading toward the beach, Terrence said.

"Your plane."

"My plane," I replied.

"Your plane," said Terrence as he took his hands and feet off the controls; for that is the proper protocol for a control handover.

Wouldn't it be grand if it was this clear who had the helm in all the other endeavors we pursue?

So here I was discovering how a small plane flies. As a long time sailor, airfoils, flow and balance were second nature to me, but like a first time freeway driver, I white-knuckled the control yoke with both hands, oversteering because I feared that without my death grip, the plane might spiral out of control—like an overpowered auto on a slippery curve.

Terrence offered the image that we flew much like an arrow, with the fletching at the rear keeping the forward weighted shaft flying a smooth trajectory. With this bit of reassurance, I relaxed. I was flying! Just a touch to the yoke angled our tail feathers and our little plane leaned into a gentle right turn toward Malibu.

The application of power to climb, the subtle changes in balance that banked us through the turns, applying a bit of trim tab and touch of rudder to counteract the torque of the propeller were quickly learned once I relaxed, understanding that the design and nature of our aircraft led it to maintain a near steady flight. The little airplane required just a touch here and there for direction and balance control to keep us on course and to correct for the gentle bumps of light air turbulence.

Learning to sail had been similar, for it was an understanding of the nature and design of sailboats, and then relaxing in my trust of that understanding so that I could find and actuate the controls for delicate balance and course adjustment. Finding the focus to coordinate helm, sail trim, and responses to the ever-changing wind and waves is best done from that relaxed state—yielding the two-fold rewards of better performance and restorative relaxation.

By reviewing portions of my professional career, I can identify many other crossroads where I held the helm well before knowing the controls. Learning on the fly was an exciting process where the goal was to find familiar handles with which to grasp unique objects and unfamiliar processes. Using past experience and trusting lessons learned from previous projects was my key to relaxing enough to feel the natural trajectory of things and gain a sensitivity for the controls.

Relaxing enough to feel how the wind blows, and track its subtle changes of force and direction is as useful at work as it is on the water. Confident in your skills and your instincts, you adjust automatically to the changing waves. You steer a smooth course, working your way along the variable fabric between wind and sea, giving all the security of a steady hand at the helm.

So enough of physics and philosophy. Let's go sailing.

Author/Inventor preparing for underwater promotional video shoot

[5.06] Diveboard - The Ultimate Gizmo

Your author is an inveterate inventor, and his development of the Diveboard makes a good story about how many factors can align to create the environment to turn a notion into a reality.

The scene was the Puerto Escondido area in the Sea of Cortez during the summer of 1999. It started when I was first towed behind a dinghy underwater wearing a dive mask and snorkel, holding on to a piece of plywood tied to a 30 foot long rope. This was a practice someone observed in the Caribbean and brought to our little community of cruising boats spending the hot months enjoying the warm clear waters with their abundant sea life. Although it felt dangerous being dragged through the water clinging on to a piece of wood, there was also an unfamiliar exhilaration as I learned to maneuver the board like a plane to dive, turn, and surface for air. The dreamlike sensation of flying underwater without self-propulsion totally captured my imagination!

Part of the magic is that breath-holding ability increases dramatically once the diver relaxes and slows his nervous heart rate. Another related sensation is that a short return to the surface for a breath or two was enough to recharge for another sustained immersion. As the relaxed body was burning little muscular energy, there was much less "oxygen debt" to repay during the surface intervals so the feeling of being "out of breath" vanished as the feeling of a new power replaced it. The reward for truly relaxing the body was to feel like you could hold your breath forever, as the dolphins seem to do when frolicking about.

The key to perfecting this experience was to reduce diver anxiety and effort, I reasoned, and so began a most interesting eighteen months.

Thinking with my sketch pad, I remembered my childhood with gas-powered model airplanes; and how precisely they could be maneuvered while flying about in a circle tethered by two slender lines that ran from a handle in the pilot's hand to a bell crank under the wing that actuated the elevators, or tail flaps, to dive and climb. The pen started to draw a flat horizontal wing with a perpendicular surface, like the stabilizing tail of a rocket. The wing and stabilizer tips became the attachment points for control lines, which could lever their respective planes to steer the device in two dimensions as the tow boat pulled you along through the third dimension.

A bit more thinking about how to attach the device to the tow rope so it would not retard free articulation yielded a bridle and pulley arrangement as shown in my original patent drawings seen below. It was then a short logical step to loop the control lines for easy diver management. On paper, I had solved all the problems, so it was time to saw wood, drill holes, select different sizes of rope, fasten it together, and recruit a towboat.

Although not yet perfected, this first model proved that minimal effort was required by the diver to control the device with the precision I remembered from my model plane days. However the greatest discovery was how the fourth dimension (time) was stretched and expanded while effortlessly flying as if a sea mammal through the warm clear fluid of my summer neighborhood.

[When you pry your eyes off this book, you can visit the website to see some video of the Diveboard in action at www.thebestgiftever.info]

With a bit of sawing and fiddling, the first prototype was ready for consumer testing and a nearby couple, he was an accomplished diver and she was much less so, were recruited as the first test subjects. Hand signals for "faster," "slower," and "stop" were worked out and we three were off to the nearby "aquarium."

He was the first to try, and steered the board into a steep dive the moment our speed got up to about three knots, and we could watch the towline swerving about as if we'd hooked a good sized fish. After more than a minute of this first dive, she became concerned he was down too long. A few seconds later, she was only partially relieved when he briefly surfaced for two breaths before resuming his underwater antics. I did not have to wait until I saw his beaming smile to know this was the right track.

She was next and his enthusiasm evaporated her fear as we gave her some simple instructions.

"First get comfortable being towed along on the surface and then try a few short dives and returns to the surface to understand how to maneuver the device," she was told. Then with her in the water and us slowly motoring away to tension the towline, he confided that she had struggled with her aquaphobia for years. When she finally signaled us to stop after several minutes of soaring about, her grin was even wider that his had been.

I was once told that curious and inventive folks find inspiration by reviewing the steps of others. Not imitating those steps but rather seeing how different ways of thinking and techniques of development build on one another until the end is fully visualized.

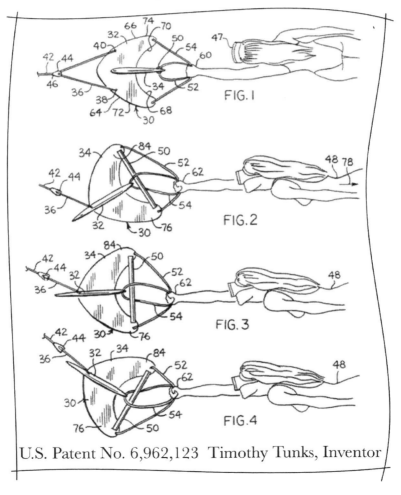

FIG. 1

FIG. 2

FIG. 3

FIG. 4

U.S. Patent No. 6,962,123   Timothy Tunks, Inventor

Tim Tunks

6

RACING

Building sailing skill and many friendships

[6.01] Ten Reasons to Race Sailboats

#1. Anything you do for yourself you should do well, for therein lies the satisfaction. Developing the skills to race sailboats well requires a substantial investment but delivers a rich variety of rewards. And please understand you need not be a champion in your fleet to race well, for the highest satisfactions come not from just beating others in competition.

If you are going to get into this wonderful sport, please bring with you an attitude that embraces learning, and the "team work" ethic of sharing common tasks with your shipmates. Managing the boat well to maximize its harvest of energy from wind and waves to propel itself toward a designated destination requires focused effort—the experience of doing this is the largest reward.

#2. Sailboat racing has a unique and wonderful social component. Sailors are social folks drawn from a wide spectrum of humanity who are most accepting of others, perhaps because the nature of the activity frequently involves *ad hoc* collections of crew from different backgrounds who can be complete strangers from one another before race day.

Rarely can you be as open and without pretense when in a common endeavor with strangers as when going out to race or just building a new sailing team.

Add to this mix the tradition of after-race hospitality and society. All the different crew from all the different boats have just completed a

72

demanding event which yields a common bond to all the participants, joining them in mutual celebration.

#3. Raising your skill levels to do things well is a rewarding process in itself. Racing is the way to measure your progress.

Without the imperative of sailing well in a race, your efforts will not be focused—you are merely out sailing (although that is tremendously rewarding in itself). And even with the whole team focused and trying their best, they need some yardstick against which to measure their efficiency. Competition not only provides that yardstick but it also provides guidance toward success with all the adjacent examples it provides.

"Look how they did that, it sure worked well for them. Let's try that ourselves next time the situation presents itself."

#4. Sharing knowledge and techniques are staples of sailboat racing society. From the Sail Master on a large boat reviewing maneuvers with his crew, to the skippers at the bar reviewing how the rules apply in a given situation, to crew on different boats exchanging tips on everything from how best to coil a line to how best to get along with an over-amped Type-A skipper. Exchanges of meaningful information become the foundation of new friendships.

#5. For sailors with families, racing can be even more rewarding than forming teams with friends and strangers.

Engaging a family in intricate cooperative teamwork is a fine bonding activity.

If you're fortunate enough to be racing in a wonderful community with lots of families, you will watch the kids forming the same sort of bonding you see with the adults as they race in their own junior classes or share duties on another parent's boat.

#6. If you are a sailboat owner, there is no better way for you to keep everything in great working order than to be out racing with some frequency. Nothing inspires you to keep your winches well lubricated like some short tacking.

#7. I teach that sailing is the art of extracting the best free ride from the forces of nature. Doing so requires both a mastery of sailing techniques—how to trim the sails, how to steer the boat, etc.—and the sensitivity to nature for correct analysis of the wind and waves. Gaining this sensitivity brings you into closer harmony with the physical world.

The art of sailing is seeing, feeling, and understanding those forces, and managing your machine to use them most efficiently. Seamanship combines that art with other skills, experience, temperament, mental strength, and a host of similar resources. Racing is a way to build your seamanship resources.

#8. There are many who enjoy competition. Some of us enjoy the tactical aspects of the game as much as we enjoy raw speed. When closely matched sailboats compete it is frequently superior tactics that win the game.

A savvy tactician has a mental projection screen on which the rules, the fleet's position, and the wind are displayed. Visualizing this information together helps the team to avoid mishaps and to occasionally turn a situation into an advantage. This part of the game can become exceedingly rewarding!

#9. For those who must invest highly in successful competition, sailboat racing has the capacity to absorb all you can invest and more. With smaller boats the financial commitment is less and you need fewer crew, but the other factors in play remain similar no matter what size the boat.

#10. And for those of us with little more to offer than our talents and our time, we can still be welcome guests and crew at yacht clubs and yachts alike. Becoming a valuable crew member can be your passport to waters you might never otherwise visit. You may find, as many have before you, that some of your closest lifelong friends are racing shipmates.

[6.02] New Year's Resolutions

Its that time again, so let's look ahead and see what we can do to ensure a great boating season.

1.   Line up crew and prepare the boat for a great racing season ahead. There is no better time to start your season's racing than the first race of the season.

2.   Start a new "Race Notebook," because there is a place for paper in your racing program. Record crew names, contact information: phone, e-mail, and "In Case of Emergency" contacts. Make notes about skill areas and levels along with any special notes like medical conditions or other physical limitations. Leave room to note tips you could offer this crew member.

The racing skipper will also make notes about the different sail settings that are best for various conditions, such as moving the genoa lead back one hole for each 2 knots of additional windspeed in the 12 to 18 knot true wind range. Note things on the boat that need attention, the names and numbers for the expert boat maintenance professionals you use, and any other important things you've learned about local conditions, any competitors you want to avoid, and anything else that will contribute to your performance on the water.

Review this notebook frequently. Making more notes is a good way to "keep your head in the game." Mental preparation is a big part of this sport.

3.   Do a thorough inspection of your sail inventory. Photograph all the sails properly trimmed and flying in appropriate wind strengths. Show them to your sailmaker when you bring your sails in for inspection and maintenance. Small things like renewing telltales, chafe patches, and securing loose stitching will add performance and longevity.

4.   Inspect and evaluate all the emergency and safety gear onboard. This starts with the First Aid Kit and carries through to the onboard tool kit. Things for plugging broken through hulls or hoses (a wax toilet bowl ring can be a boat saver as it conforms to any shape hole), and other critical spares like bilge pump fuses should be properly packaged and conveniently located near their place of need. Include the VHF radio and GPS in your emergency planning. Imagine an inexperienced operator communicating critical position information when all other hands are engaged in dealing with an onboard emergency. This will guide you in creating posted operation instructions. Include an easily read "Radio Operation" card identifying the vessel by name, type, CF or other registration numbers, along with sail numbers and any easily

seen vessel identification—this will help this operator clearly state information when requested. A dedicated notepad and attached pencil makes recording things like Latitude/Longitude position numbers an easy and accurate process.

5.   Inspect all the "Turning Bits" and "Juicy Joints." This means squeeze all the hoses to find soft spots while looking for chafe. Check all the hose clamps, and operate all the seacocks. Any signs of water pumps leaking are best addressed immediately to prevent bearing damage or catastrophic failure at an inopportune time.

Experienced engineers frequently use such opportunities to place the spare pump, alternator, or whatever into service during the inspection. A multitude of benefits are gained: you know that the spare fits and works, you know how to fit the replacement, and the replaced part is exposed for a detailed inspection to see if it needs service to remain a reliable spare.

Inspect for oily tracks around the engine and transmission. Tightening a filter or loose fitting, locating a failing sender, or any other potential leak, can be a small investment with a huge payoff in expenses avoided.

6.   I know this looks like a lot of work so far, but here is one more big job that pays off in many different ways—Empty the Boat! With all the sails at your sailmaker for service, you are well started on a project to empty all the seat lockers, drawers, cupboards, crooks, and nannies.

With an empty boat, cleaning is easy and you can thoughtfully distribute the things you need, where you need them, and be confident that they have been inspected. With vacuum and sponge you can remove all the fluff and stuff that clogs bilge pumps and 'limber holes" (the name for the holes and gaps in the bottom corners of lockers that route water down to the bilge). You also get a clean slate on which you can trace future drips and difficulties.

The empty boat gives you the best access to follow the hoses and wires that snake through your empty lockers. Early discovery of how the spare anchor chain chafes the bilge pump wires can prevent all sorts of mischief.

Once you've seen all that stuff spread out on the dock, you can sort what goes back on the boat, what goes home, and what goes into the dumpster or by the gangway for recycling.

7.   Have a crew party. Maybe have a dock party when you empty the boat. This involves the whole crew in getting to know the boat from the inside out while spreading the work load. Bonding the crew to the boat is one of the most valuable accomplishments you can achieve and well worth the effort.

Most of these resolutions work for non-racing boaters and crew too. A better prepared crew bonded with the boat, the skipper, and each other make for a rewarding boating season.

[6.03] Crew and Boat as a System

Sometimes I think of crew training as building a team to sail the boat, however I've been thinking more about considering the larger "system" of boat, skipper, and crew interacting as an organic whole to wind, water, and competition.

The catalyst for this new thinking about humans, machines (the boat and all its parts), water, and wind as a coherent system was a discussion with the mainsail trimmer during the last reaching leg of a shifty-winded race. He was attentive to the sail's reaction to the wind, trimming in as it luffed and trimming out as the leach tell tales stalled, but I could not convince him to proactively over trim a bit to help keep the slot between main and genoa open when the apparent wind went forward during the lulls between the puffs.

When I'd ask for a proactive trim, he would inform me with a growl that the main looked just fine. The difficulty was that he was not considering the total system from his limited point of view.

My vantage point allowed me to see much more. I could easily see the shape and size of the slot as sails were trimmed in and out and I could see a lot more. Looking ahead a bit, the puffs and lulls were clearly visible on the water and in the behavior of the boats ahead. I could also look around to see when we'd encounter disturbed air with its diminished power for our sails and when we'd emerge into clear air again.

Seeing the whole system gave me a picture of all the elements interacting which enabled a higher level of anticipation for how the helm and crew should respond to the changing conditions—trimming the sails just a bit earlier so they were already in the proper configuration to encounter the new wind, generating increased drive to inch away from the competition.

Broadening the focus to consider the fastest line to the finish enables a better management of this system, enabling good decisions about where the light wind spots would be so we could plan to sail a bit higher, generating more apparent wind in those light spots, and then when the wind puffs up a bit, ride the increased wind down to a lower, more direct course to the mark. We could utilize that fast line to our advantage by watching our nearby competitors luffing each other upwards in the puffs which in turn leaves them to sail more slowly downward to clear the next buoy. Understanding how the adjacent boats will behave enables us to better choose our defensive and offensive tactics.

Bringing this all back to the mainsail trimmer, we see how important it is to look ahead of the immediate moment when airflow over his sail changes. He should anticipate what he must do to adjust the slot—the genoa encounters the new apparent wind before the mainsail because it is in front. Avoiding that moment of inefficiency, when the slot closes as the genoa is first trimmed in for a lull, can maintain enough drive sometimes to pass a less well-trimmed boat. The mainsail trimmer needs to monitor the genoa trimmer—not just his mainsail—to proactively trim the main to provide consistent maximum drive.

There are a few different approaches to encourage this expanded notion of individual crew activities coordinating with wind, water, course, and competition as a coherent system. A good starting point might be emphasizing the notion that the primary crew focus needs to be keeping the sails driving as best they can for as much time as possible by minimizing the periods they are not in ideal shape. Things like minimizing transition time when the weather mark is rounded, the spinnaker raised, the pole properly positioned, the new sail trimmed as the genoa is dropped or rolled up to improve the flow of undisturbed air are obvious, and can be improved with drilling the individual activities of each person onboard. But awareness of systematic subtleties involved in managing the shifty reach through traffic doesn't come from drilling skills.

All aboard need to picture how the entire system is behaving at the moment and how it should adapt to the next change in condition. The helmsman and the spinnaker trimmer can coordinate to maximize efficient use of wave energy down wind, but boat speed will be improved if the mainsail and the spinnaker pole trim are also well managed.

In the next few races I'll try to increase crew awareness of the total system as they execute their individual duties, prioritizing the things that maintain maximum drive from the sails and anticipating the adaptations and maneuvers to come.

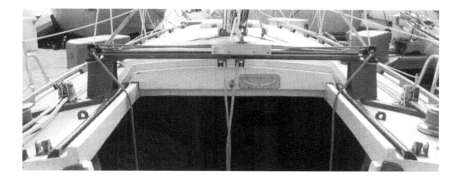

[6.04] Upgrade your Traveler for Better Driving

"Why is this so valuable?" you may ask.

Driving a well canvased sloop on a beat, the boat can be easily overpowered in the puffs of stronger wind, and develop "weather helm" quickly as the boat tries to round up—turning toward the wind. With convenient and easily operated traveler control lines, the mainsail can be eased down to give immediate relief at the first sign of increasing wind pressure.

Traveling down allows the boat to accelerate, gaining a little jump ahead and to weather of boats not reacting as quickly. The alternative of easing the mainsheet opens the mainsail leech with a resultant loss of power (unless a powerful vang is set to prevent the boom from rising). Driving to weather becomes as much a matter of playing the traveler as playing the tiller in puffy wind conditions.

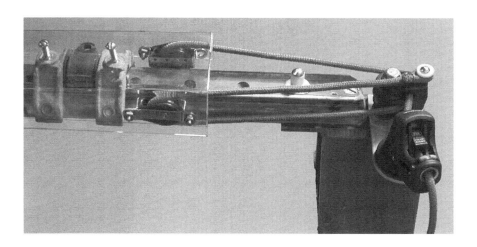

Replacing original non-bearing blocks and bullseye fairleads, which provide large measures of system friction, and installing these new **PXR** Spinlock swivel cleats (a simple flick of the line upward releases while a light flick downward locks this little wonder) makes for a superior rigging upgrade to classic racer/cruisers.

The photo above of our upgrade also shows the relocated vang and Cunningham lines going through Lance Cleats mounted on the underside of the traveler giving the pit/main trimmer perfect access and leverage. The old fairleads and the control line Lance Cleats are seen on either side of the companionway hatch slide track. Also shown on the following page is the clear plastic study model I made to work out details before starting to machine aluminum.

[6.05] Starting First Timers

I participate in many educational events and one thing we always do is have a little safety talk whenever there are new sailors being introduced to race boats. All boat owners have some routine to make new guests or crew safe and comfortable The better that routine is, the safer and more comfortable the newbies on board will be.

Here is what I said to a class of fifty newbies being introduced to the sport of sailboat racing. I try to make these same points when I'm aboard a racing boat.

Sailing is lots of fun and some of the best times of my life happened while I was on the water. However sailing is not quite the same as a Disney ride with its attendants standing by should any mishap occur.

The first safety rule is that you're much safer on the boat than in the water—so stay on the boat! "One hand for you and one hand for the ship" is the old saw that reminds you not to lose your grip on the boat while you are performing some task.

All boats should have plenty of Personal Flotation Devices onboard, so please feel free to wear one if you are a non-swimmer or have other concerns. If you feel more secure wearing a PFD, go ahead and buy your own so you can always wear it. New styles are comfortable and much less bulky than the borrowed ones you are likely to encounter.

Sun overexposure can easily become an issue. You are out in the sun with plenty of water and other reflective surfaces to bounce harmful U.V. rays up onto usually shaded skin surfaces. As your mom would do, I want to remind you to use your sunblock and wear your hat. Skin damage is a worse penalty than hat hair.

"Most every part of the boat is harder than most every part of you." Try not to bump into stuff and try very hard not to bump others into stuff. The boat rocks from side to side and waves can bounce you in unexpected directions. It is perfectly okay to balance yourself with a grip on someone's knee or shoulder. Losing your balance can land you on an unsuspecting crew mate, so a quick grab—even if it's personal—is preferable to the full crash.

"Sometimes he who does nothing helps most." A small sailboat is a crowded place and it is easy to be in the way. Sometimes someone will be performing a task and your instinct is to step up and help; and sometimes that's a good thing.

However, the more frequent situation is that your move to assist someone who does not need your assistance places you unexpectedly into the path of another crew doing something else. You will slowly acclimate to this as you watch things happen and listen to the crew boss or skipper who is directing activities. Listening and being attentive can be difficult in unfamiliar environments so try to adjust your focus.

Make sure to enjoy the sights and sounds around you. Take in the graceful shapes of the sails as they bend the wind, powering the boat through the water. But still remain alert to instructions and clues as to what might soon be expected of you.

Sometimes you will not remember the names of some of your fellow crew when you need to communicate. It is perfectly acceptable to touch a shoulder or grab an elbow to start a conversation or deliver a message.

Make the best of a "Dock Work" introduction to see what it's like moving about on the boat before it shoves off. Get a sense of what parts of the boat will be useful for handholds when the boat is bouncing about crowded with your mates. Figure out the various paths crew can take while shifting from side to side as the boat tacks.

Sailors worship the wind the way bankers worship money, so start being aware of the wind yourself. All sailboats should have a wind indicator on the top of the mast, and it points to where the apparent wind is coming from. Your awareness of the winds force and direction helps you raise your general understanding of what's happening.

Every master sailor has an intimate relationship with the wind, with expertise at not only reading its present energy and direction but also reading the clues about what's to come.

When the wind is coming from behind you, the boat is upright, the wind velocity drops, it gets warmer, and you want to take off your jacket. With the wind behind, you can generally sail more directly to your destination. When you are "beating" into the wind, the boat leans over, you feel the apparent wind velocity increase, and the boat has to tack back and forth to go upwind. Tacking will be one of the first maneuvers you practice.

When tacking, the sails move from one side of the boat to the other, which involves releasing one line, the old "working" jib sheet, and then pulling in on the new working sheet. The crew are mostly sitting on the high side of the boat while beating, to help balance against the force of the wind leaning the boat. Besides the valuable ballast contribution these crew make just sitting there, they also keep a look-out for kelp and other objects in the water while they remain alert and prepared for the next maneuver.

During the transition between one tack and the other is when lots of things happen, all of which should be well coordinated. Sails are shifting from one side of the boat to the other as the crew are moving in the opposite direction. Sheets (the ropes tied to the sail's "clew." as that corner of the sail is named, are called sheets) must be left free to run without tangles on feet, arms, other body parts, or other things on the boat. The opposite sheet must be hauled in; first with direct pulling and finally with the assistance of a winch's cranking power.

Practice with the winch handle, as it can be tricky inserting and removing it. Be careful with these handles as they resemble expensive hammers that do not float. And like hammers, they can be dangerous if they flail about in the hands of a stumbling crew. Likewise they can slip out if not fully inserted into the winch, being at least an embarrassment and at most a danger to all.

Moving from side to side on a heeling (that's the term for leaning) sailboat is not always easy, so help yourself by figuring out good paths to travel. Discuss with your adjacent crew how best to coordinate your moves. Don't be shy—communicate. Building an effective team is a big part of sailing success and one of the big personal rewards; it feels good to work out cooperative methods. Communicating freely promotes effective crew work as well as rewarding relationships.

Performing activities at the dock gives you a chance to stop and work things out. Many maneuvers are much more difficult to pause and work out once you are sailing. Your goal is to help new crew feel comfortable on the boat as they perform their various tasks.

Minor injuries can happen when the breeze is up and the water is rough. The most frequent injuries include bumped knees and elbows, small hand cuts and scrapes from unfriendly handholds, and bumps on the head from the boom—that's why they call it a boom—during a tack. Gloves and knee pads will help protect from injuries and also enable the wearer to function more effectively. Some experienced race boat owners keep some spare gloves, knee pads, and foul weather gear aboard just for this purpose.

Lastly, here is the drill if someone does manage to transport themselves off the boat and into the water. It is highly unlikely you will get a chance to practice this today, but do rehearse it a bit in your mind so you can be prepared.

Whoever first sees someone go over hails loud and clear, "Man Overboard" and points his arm and finger directly at the person in the water. This person is the "Spotter" and keeps the swimmer or MOB in sight every second until the MOB is recovered or another Spotter relieves him. This pointing is most important, for it permits the other crew to know the MOB's position while still doing the boat handling duties required to return and retrieve.

So stay on the boat, try not to bump things and people too hard, look out for sharp stuff, converse to coordinate your activities, act thoughtfully, and have fun.

These are the things I say to newbies to help them have a safe and rewarding experience.

The goal is not to sail the boat,

but rather to help the boat sail herself.

Visualize and anticipate - for safety and fun

The start is your first opportunity to win the race.
Don't waste it.

Some Start Line Basics

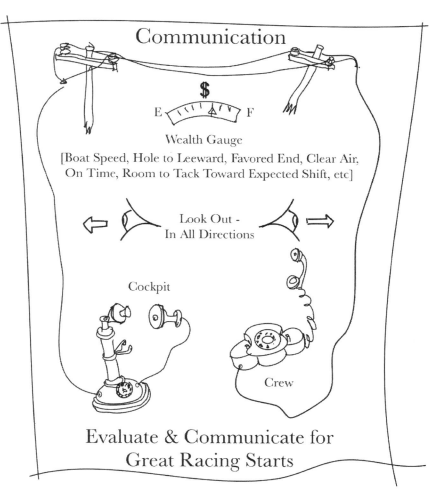

Communication

$

E ⌐ ⌐ ⌐ △ ⌐ ⌐ F

Wealth Gauge

[Boat Speed, Hole to Leeward, Favored End, Clear Air,
On Time, Room to Tack Toward Expected Shift, etc]

Look Out -
In All Directions

Cockpit

Crew

Evaluate & Communicate for
Great Racing Starts

Take some time to polish your skills with practice drills.
Some parts of the start to think about:

[6.06] Communication and Wealth Management
For Better Starts

Hitting the line at full speed, on time, at the favored end with a good hole to leeward is your goal. Listed below are some skills and drills to help achieve that goal

Boat Handling

When you become a competitive racer, there are two important maneuvers you need to master—how to quickly return to the pre-start side of the line after an "Over Early," and how to best execute "Penalty Turns," the penance you can usually pay for forgiveness and redemption (exoneration of a foul).   Practice with these maneuvers will help the whole crew work as a team to make efficient and timely adjustments to maintain boat speed as the helmsman drives the boat. Note how long it takes to regain full speed. Superior ability to time and perform efficient maneuvers can be a huge tactical advantage during prestart jockeying for position. And think about how valuable good boat handling skills will be if you become involved in a "man overboard" recovery situation!

Judging Time, Distance and Speed

Some folks are naturally good at this while others must work hard to get good.   Invent practice drills that involve the whole crew—for example, pick a mark within a minute or two of sailing time, and sail toward it at top speed and have each crew write a guess as to how long it will take to fetch it.

Controlling Speed

Do the same exercise, except this time sail to within about two minutes distance from the mark, and control your speed to get you there in exactly three minutes. Practice quickly slowing the boat and then re-trim to gain your speed back. See how long this takes at various points of sail in various wind conditions.   Do turns and "whoop de dos" (large rapid rudder movements) to burn off speed, then trim and drive for best acceleration. Repeat as necessary! You can never get too good at this. Knowing when you need to "burn off" time on the way to the line, and being able to judge when to slow the boat and leave enough time to get back up to speed are the skills you seek.

Important Note: Most cruising and novice class starts are not fiercely contested. Getting to the favored end of the line, on time and at full speed will win you the start in most of your races. First master those skills before engaging in tactical games with your competition. Those can come later when you are more perfect in your speed and distance judgements. What good is it to battle with a single competitor while the fleet sails away?

Maneuvering in Close Proximity of Other Boats

The skilled skipper has confidence in his ability to control his boat's course and speed. It is confidence gained through practice and experience, providing comfort in the knowledge you can react correctly when boats get close.

There is nothing as good as another boat of about the same speed and handling characteristics as yours with whom you can sail to compare performance. With a familiar sailing partner, you will become comfortable sailing in close proximity.

Understanding the Racing Rules of Sailing and How they Apply

The uniform set of racing rules that govern most U.S. and international racing are called the "RRS" in the "Sailing Instructions," and any modifications of those rules for a specific event must specifically reference the RRS rule that is being modified. The *Rules* of sailboat racing are much simpler today than they were in the last century, and most of them are common sense. Companions to the *Rules* are the *Appeals and Cases* where important situations are described in detail, with clear explanations about how the *Rules* apply. One fun exercise is to sit around a large table with the model boats the club uses for protest hearings, and to re-enact some of the cases that apply to situations you have encountered.

Now go sailing and have fun working on your skill sets and your teamwork. And please don't forget to enjoy all the magic that can be found from time out on the water.

However:
First at the start, first at the weather mark, first to finish—
The first two don't count.

[6.07] Learning Seamanship from RacingTragedies

Seamanship is the combination of art, skill, and experience which the accomplished sailor uses for safe and efficient operation of a vessel. When something goes seriously awry superior seamanship can frequently be the factor that keeps an accident from turning into a tragedy. But how does a racing sailor build a reserve of seamanship so his account is sufficient for extreme situations?

Racers have finely honed sailing skills and the successful ones have sharpened their skill sets to a ravor edge. But there is a large segment of seamanship that racers don't experience.

My mentor Hank used to say, "Experience is what you get right after when you need it." A lesson is learned but a price is paid. However, vicarious experience can offer similar value without the physical involvement, and most importantly, it can be acquired in quantity and banked for future need.

I was a very active Ham radio operator during my decade sailing about Mexico, and emergency communications are a most important part of Ham radio. The backstay antenna on my boat emerged through a gap in the solar panels, providing a most effective ground plane, which gave me a "Big Signal" frequently heard when others were too weak. This put me in the center of lots of emergency communications.

Mentioned in a past chapter was visualization's usefulness in radio communication. The ability to visualize and put oneself into the whole situation renders a global view of the various factors involved. Experiences visualized during radio communications gave me a substantial reserve of vicarious experience—experience that I try to exercise whenever possible.

There was a recent tragic loss of life when one sailor from the experienced crew of six aboard *Uncontrollable Urge* perished during The Islands Race in 2013. The boat went aground because a rudder failure rendered the boat uncontrollable in large seas near San Clemente Island. According to *Latitude 38*, the crew launched their life raft after anchoring attempts failed to keep the boat off the rocky lee shore. Crewman Craig Thomas Williams, 38, did not survive. Our hearts go out to his family and friends. Can we honor that loss by vicariously experiencing aspects of this tragedy to build our own seamanship skills? Let's try.

Experienced sailors know a myriad of ways to deal with a rudder failure, and *Uncontrollable Urge*'s crew were all experienced sailors. This crew had plenty of confidence they could deal with the emergency, informing the Coast Guard and others monitoring the situation that they would arrange for a private service to dispatch a rescue tow boat. As considerate racers, they didn't want to disturb the race for others. As it turns out the tow boat was never launched because of the difficult conditions.

How could things have been different? Race boats have broken rudders many times with mostly less tragic results because a full crew of accomplished sailors finds a way to stabilize the situation. The skipper and crew of their previous boat named *Uncontrollable Urge* had managed an earlier rudder failure on that boat, which likely gave them increased confidence they could successfully manage this situation.

Many sailboats can be steered effectively using the sails and jury-rigged rudders or towing a warp that can be moved athwartship to drag the stern in one direction or the other. This common knowledge could lead to seamanship failure because that knowledge doesn't recognize how differently a modern lightweight racer with its keel ballast bulb hung from a narrow blade performs with its minimal directional stability. Previous successes give us confidence facing present challenges, but that confidence can be dangerous if not tempered with knowledge of problems others have had in similar situations.

I vicariously experienced Nick Barran's emergency as he told his story of a lost rudder on a similarly keeled 40 footer a few days out from Hawaii. Nick's sophisticated analysis of the problem focuses on the difficulty of keeping the sail's center of effort over the boat's greatly reduced center of lateral resistance. Without the straight tracking force of the rudder at the transom, that reduced center of lateral resistance moves forward in the boat, compounding difficulties of maintaining balance and steerage speed needed for effective function of jury-rigged devices.

Nick said they could get the boat moving with careful trimming of sails and heel angle, but as soon as a wave rolled the boat one way or another, the sail's center of effort would move to one side or the other — spinning the boat end for end around the pivot point of the narrow keel's center of lateral resistance. As soon as details of the *Urge*'s tragedy were released, the image of Nick's boat spinning out came to mind. Remembering large confused seas I've experienced near islands helped me realize how much more difficult it must have been for this crew than Nick's in his more regular offshore seas.

All race boats are required to carry anchoring gear appropriate to their size (racing dinghies excepted), but no serious competitor carries more weight than they absolutely have to. This means the absolute minimum anchor is the standard.

My guess is that *Uncontrollable Urge* had a lightweight burying type anchor with light rode and some chain, which could hold the boat if properly buried in accommodating bottom conditions with a chafe protected bridle secured to substantial bow cleats. The rocky bottom of the San Clemente shoreline is not such an accommodating bottom because any momentary hook the anchor does gets on a rock or in a crevice can be quickly yanked out as the rode slacks on the rebound from a large wave with no help from a long and heavy shot of chain to hold the anchor down. Few race boats are properly set up with bridles and fairleads to sturdy cleats to prevent chafe from quickly parting a slender rode lead from a bouncing bow, let alone robust anchors and ample chain for security in big waves. (Lack of elasticity in modern cordage makes for lousy anchor rode, so spare spinnaker sheets or halyards are a poor substitute for enough rode to provide sufficient scope.)

Racers seldom if ever find need to anchor in situations that cruisers frequently experience, so how were these racers to know their backup plan was so frail? Should more race crews take the boat out for a bit of cruising to see how their anchoring gear and skills measure up, or attend cruiser's seamanship seminars?

Finding your way to dry land through breaking surf on a rocky shore is a dicey thing even if you are an accomplished free diver with swim fins, mask, snorkel, and some protection from your gloves and wetsuit. I've been there. Getting safely to shore bobbing in large confused surf without control because of a bulky life jacket is orders of magnitude more dicey. My actual experience could be your vicarious experience. Those on *Uncontrollable Urge* may have had the same knowledge, but I wish someone in their communication net had emphasized that specific danger when the boat first reported it was disabled. Could additional weight of that hazard have tipped the scales toward seeking immediate emergency rescue in spite of the possibility of losing the boat?

Had their experiences been different this race crew might have made different decisions leading to a better outcome. We cannot know. But their experiences taught them to believe they could save themselves and their new race boat—so they passed on what turned out to be their last chance for a safe rescue from nearby competitors.

Just like compromises in deciding how heavy to build the rudder system or how heavy the ground tackle should be, there are compromises in which experiences a racer seeks out. It takes a lot of time, money and effort to develop your "chops" as a racer, and the same goes for learning seamanship.

How does the diligent sailor budget his sailing time and money between building racing skills and building seamanship skills? If competition and bragging rights loom large in your priorities, might you not be tempted to scrimp on seamanship to lavish more on racing?

One lesson to pick up is that windy snotty conditions should be embraced as an opportunity to go sailing. Next time a race is cancelled because of big wind and seas, consider taking the crew out anyhow. See what happens to you, the crew, and the boat in difficult conditions. However, start that testing very close to your home port so you can bail for familiar shelter if something or someone has a failure.

Another lesson is listen to stories and read articles to learn what can happen. Then mentally rehearse those scenarios and decide how you might respond.

Let us all share our experiences with one another to elevate our levels of seamanship. The last thing we racers want is for some outside authority to devise classes and tests and certifications to prove we are safe.

Rehearsal is Preparation and Preparation is Precaution.
Scallywag racing to San Diego 7/4/91

7

TIPS, TOOLS, & TECHNIQUES

[7.01] Fluid Transfer

Back in my teenage years some kids' cars carried a length of hose long enough to reach through the filler cap to the bottom of an automobile fuel tank with the other end stuck in a container set on the ground. As you've no doubt deduced, this hose was used for acquiring gasoline and you may even remember the taste from your first mouthful when suck-starting such a siphon.

There are better ways.

Hauling and transferring fluids was a basic part of cruising Mexico in 1990. Fuel in Cabo San Lucas came from the Pemex station on the edge of town, next to the immigration office where you filled your jugs and caught a taxi back to the dinghy dock. You eventually made it back to your boat, rolling in the outer anchorage where no funnel was large enough to catch all the fuel you'd pour toward your tank.

"You can learn something new every day as long as you aren't too stupid," my grandfather advised.

I developed the following trick after watching the fuel supply guy in Zihuatanejo siphon outboard fuel from the full jugs in his pick-up to the empty ones the fishermen presented at quayside.

Here is some science: a gravity siphon will run once air has been expelled from the tube and will continue to run as long as the receiving container is lower than the fluid level in the supply container. To start the siphon flow, the pressure at the outlet end of the hose must be lower than the supply end, and that is how the sucking start became the standard in my youth.

The Zihuatanejo fuel guy inverted our process by *increasing* the air pressure inside the supply jug instead of *reducing* the pressure in the hose as we did with our suck-start. His technique was to seal the hose in the neck of the plastic supply jug with his hand while he gave the jug a sudden powerful hug to compress the container, increasing the internal air pressure enough to force the fuel up through the hose and start the siphon action.

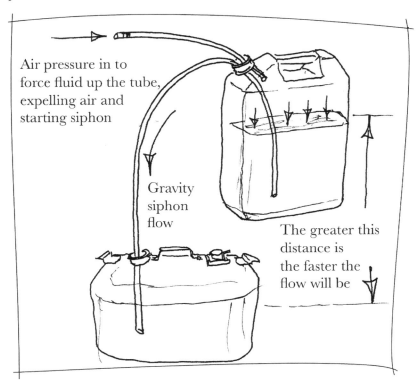

Air pressure in to force fluid up the tube, expelling air and starting siphon

Gravity siphon flow

The greater this distance is the faster the flow will be

However the hug start is less effective when the container is only partially filled because there is a far larger volume of air to compress. This difficulty lead me to an alternative for increasing pressure in the supply container to start the siphon—blow into it.

My first attempt had me sealing the siphon hose into the supply container with two cupped hands leaving a small gap to blow into. One big breath was sufficient to get the last two gallons from a five gallon jug.

How much simpler and cleaner siphoning was compared to pouring through a funnel on a rocking boat at anchor.

But this technique brought my mouth and face right up to the fuel vapors, triggering unwelcome memories of my youth. One more element was required to reach the final elegant solution and that was the *blow hose*. One end was placed along the siphon hose just inside the neck of the supply vessel and sealed by hand or wrapped rag. Using this blow hose, face and nose could now be out of range of noxious vapors and the blow could be delivered from a greater distance while striking a more dignified pose.

The last step was to make a tape ring around one end of the blow hose to identify which end was the mouthpiece when the hose was retrieved from its Zip-loc storage bag. I continued to use this fluid transfer tool for the next decade and swear by its use.

[7.02] Taming the Gimbaled Stove

Living full time on a sailboat that sails around much of the year, and spending lots of time in bouncy remote anchorages changes your perspective in many ways. This story is about the gimbaled galley stove that swings athwartship (from side to side in the boat) so that it can remain level as the boat heels or rolls. This is important to keep the soup pot from spilling and to bake the bread into a nice symmetrical loaf.

Swinging is an obvious virtue for cooking on the tilt, but it adds its complications—inertia of motion being a big one and balance being another.

To understand the balance issue, imagine the stove hanging level from its two pivots, one on either side close to the top (see drawing on next page). The very bottom of the stove is frequently weighted so that the imbalance of a stove top pot being off center is somewhat mitigated. However this picture changes drastically when the oven door is opened, moving the stove's center of gravity toward the front. Unless the cook has Olympian acrobatic skills, supporting the open door to keep the swinging stove level while checking the lasagna and dealing with a bouncing boat is fraught with danger.

The inertia issue is described by Newton's first law of motion: "A body in motion tends to stay in motion." In this case the law refers to the tendency of the stove's initial swing to level itself, gaining enough momentum to swing the stove past level.   This *over-swing* can be reinforced with a properly timed roll of the boat, throwing even the best anchored pan off the burner or the baked fish onto the floor.

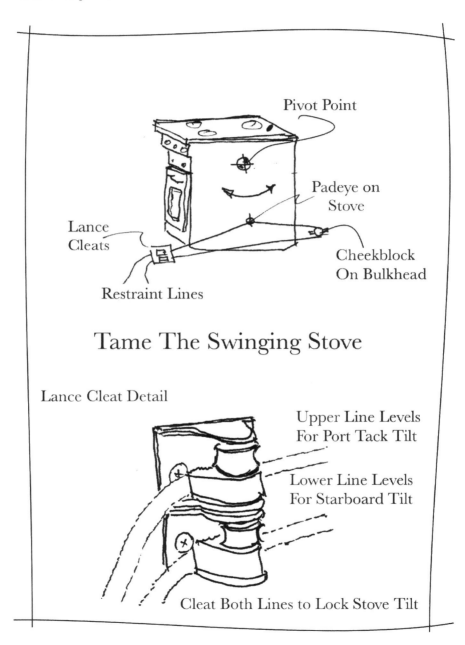

Pivot Point

Padeye on Stove

Lance Cleats

Cheekblock On Bulkhead

Restraint Lines

Tame The Swinging Stove

Lance Cleat Detail

Upper Line Levels For Port Tack Tilt

Lower Line Levels For Starboard Tilt

Cleat Both Lines to Lock Stove Tilt

The last situation I'll ask you to imagine is making a long upwind sailboat passage, where the boat is never on the level. Every normally flat galley counter is now a slick inclined ramp ill-suited for construction of even sandwich meals, so the cutting board atop the stove becomes prime real estate at sea. Balance and inertia are both at play in this situation as you seek a level and locked work surface.

Here's the "leash" system I devised for *Scallywag*. The fully adjustable restraint this line and cleat arrangement offers is vastly superior to the common barrel bolt option which locks the stove in just a few fixed positions.

[7.03] The Straight Poop

When *Scallywag* returned to suburban life from her "decade at large" in Mexico's western waters, it was time to rework her head waste discharge system. Long experience with plumbing failures on other boats set me out to engineer the best possible holding tank, and under the guidance of Marina del Rey boat genius Eric Lambert—we did it.

. My hope is that understanding the processes we went through to install "The Straight Poop" will inform your own approaches to problem solving on your boat and elsewhere in life.

Step #1 Analyze the System:

Leaking, Plugging, Smelling, and Pump Problems—
Four Arch Enemies of Head Happiness

My early sailing mentor Hank McGill's "First Rule of Plumbing" states: "More pieces = more joints = more leaks." which tells us "the simpler the better." When you compare alternatives, count the number of components required for each alternative and note the serviceability of each component.

Keeping the ocean out of the boat is preserved in many systems with an "Air Gap" or vented loop—a frequent accomplice to the "Plugging Bandit," for it is the bottleneck in the system, un-handily located in the middle of things. In our system the smallest restriction is at the beginning, assuring a smooth passage to the destination.

"Whiffy Head" comes mostly from smelly anaerobic bacteria that live in oxygen-starved environments—aerobic bacteria live in oxygen-rich environments and don't smell bad. Plenty of air in anyplace where seawater and human waste loiter makes a huge difference in bouquet — either starve them of sea water by using the boat's freshwater supply for flushing, or gas them with oxygen. Do both and you'll have the head your sailor friends will envy

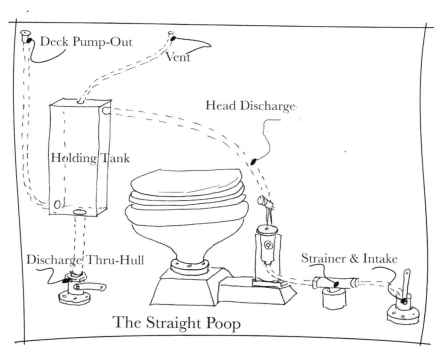

The Straight Poop

With the holding tank thru-hull opened, seawater surges up the discharge hose and into the bottom of the tank with each roll of the boat.

This surge and retreat flushes the tank bottom and circulates fresh air through the vent, giving you an oxygen-rich environment for the jolly little aerobic guys.

"Hank's Second Rule" tells us that pumps clog, leak, and break down. "That's how you know it's a pump, Matey." The fewer pumps the better and put them where you can service them. Design so that an electrical failure won't generate a sanitary catastrophe. "If seawater and electricity were meant to cohabit, we could run the wires on the outside of the boat." [Hank's Third Rule]

Step #2 Research to understand alternatives.

My epiphany came while inspecting a Beneteau. Here's the trick.

A. Locate the holding tank above the water line in a location where it can gravity-drain out through the hull seacock. Closing that seacock prevents discharge where not permitted, opening it in "discharge permitted" waters empties the tank. Provide a short, direct path from the head discharge to the top of the holding tank. Making both the tank drain and through-hull fitting a size larger than the head discharge hose insures a smooth departure of any solids. The vented tank provides you with a clog-proof vented loop to prevent seawater from back siphoning into the bowl.

B. Provide excellent air venting to the tank, which facilitates the tank's "breathing" as the water surges in and out.

C. Locate the tank's pump-out at the lowest point possible, with the shortest and most direct path to the deck fitting.

Step #3 Fit the plan to your application.

Here is where the fun starts. Each decision involves some sort of compromise. You want to make certain the compromises don't multiply one another. You may find the perfect solution through dumb luck or factors that pre-empt alternatives. More likely, you will have to keep an open enough mind to examine many alternatives and compare them without prejudice—not that easy, considering the human trait of falling in love with some detail while missing significant larger issues.

The Best Way to Clean Innards and Keep Parts Slippery

Muriatic acid in low concentrations can be found in hardware stores around the world and many other places as well. H-Cl (Hydrochloric Acid) is what you can ask for if you want to see if the clerk remembers any high school chemistry.

As the head is flushed with sea water, the inside of the discharge plumbing becomes coated with a build up of salts and other material. Toilet paper fibers can embed to make a cement-like coating. Low concentration Hydrochloric Acid dissolves this build-up, and regular use will keep your discharge hoses clean and clog-free.

Important note: *Add acid to water and never add water to acid.* Why? Because it blows up!—another really important thing to remember. We are going to do just that by sending acid into your discharge hose, past the joker valve (the one way flapper valve at the pump discharge), and then we will add flush water to use some of that explosive energy inside the hose to attack the build-up.

The treatment procedure is to first pump the bowl dry. Do this in "discharge permitted" waters. (Important note: With a holding tank set up with diverter valves, you should bypass the tank for direct overboard discharge to avoid possible pressure build up in the tank) You then pour in about a cup of the acid, and pump the bowl dry. Then open the flush intake on the head, and pump to flush, sending the mixture into the discharge hose. Watch it bubble and maybe even smoke a bit, but be careful. A bubble bursting and sending droplets of acid into your eyeball would certainly spoil your day! Gloves, safety goggles, and protective clothing are the uniform for this duty.

When the bubbling subsides, pump lots of times to flush the deposits out of the hoses and out the thru-hull. If there was lots of bubbling it means the deposits are abundant which will suggest that you repeat this procedure a time or two, depending how thick the coating is inside the discharge part of your system. Try to visualize the salts caking the hose and position your mass of bubbling acid to do the most good. A bit of bowl brushing toward the end of the bubbling and into the flushing phases will remove discoloration and deposits there.

When finished with the acid treatment, it's time to lube the moving parts. The pump shaft is usually exposed when the handle is up and can be easily lubed with a bit of silicone or other waterproof grease. Failure to do this over time results in seawater spurting out when you pump because the shaft seal wears out for lack of lubrication.

The interior seals and valves are lubricated with water-soluble cutting oil like machinists and pipe threaders use. A gallon lasted me over twenty years, including gifting lots of small bottles to friends made during during my Mexican decade. If you keep a few ounces in a sealable squeeze bottle, it is easy to add a few drops to the bowl whenever the pump feels stiff or makes noises.

Some boaters add a lube-injection tee valve into the intake hose so that a bit of lube is added with every flush. I had such a "lube injector" for several years but then removed it for simplicity and suffered no loss as long as I added a few drops of oil into the bowl from time to time.

The squeaky head gets some lube

Explanations for Guests

Many cute placards are available explaining that anything going into the bowl should pass through a human first. Then there will be a discrete bin for used paper close at hand. World travelers are used to such a protocol, but to others the practice may seem a bit yucky. I kept a roll of paper towels handy in the head—useful for bundling stuff into a more attractive discard package so it's less likely to offend anyone.

However, my well-maintained system with a Raritan PH-II head swallowed toilet paper with ease for many years—as long as flushing water was pumped vigorously when paper was deposited. Whatever the case with your system, do post approved procedures to the guests.

You may have read "Men at sea sit to pee" somewhere and it is a very worthwhile practice, especially for your guests who are not used to unexpected motions of the boat. Unless you enjoy washing up splashes of urine around the head, legislating this slogan as the approved practice aboard will make your life better. It's the manly way!

Lastly you might explain that privacy on a boat is a matter of mind over ears and noses. What we must do, we do—and we extend that privilege to all our shipmates. We just imagine that the walls and doors are thicker and carry on without fuss.

[7.04] *Fusing Dacron Yacht Braid Rope Ends*

Finishing line ends can be a tedious task, but if not properly whipped, unsightly "Irish Pennants"—as frayed line ends were called by 19th Century seamen—are the result.

Frayed and unravelling rope ends can be found around most any boat but you won't find them on anything from rigger Stan Harris' hands. Stan's "deep cross fusing" technique solidifies the end of double braid line like nothing I've seen before. Although not applicable to Spectra and some of the newest low-stretch fibers, this solution is the best I've seen for our common synthetics that melt and fuse well.

The secret of this technique is to twice slice deeply with the hot knife into the line's end to create a large mass of deeply fused fiber that can withstand weathering and physical impact.

Fusing Dacron Yachtbraid Line Ends

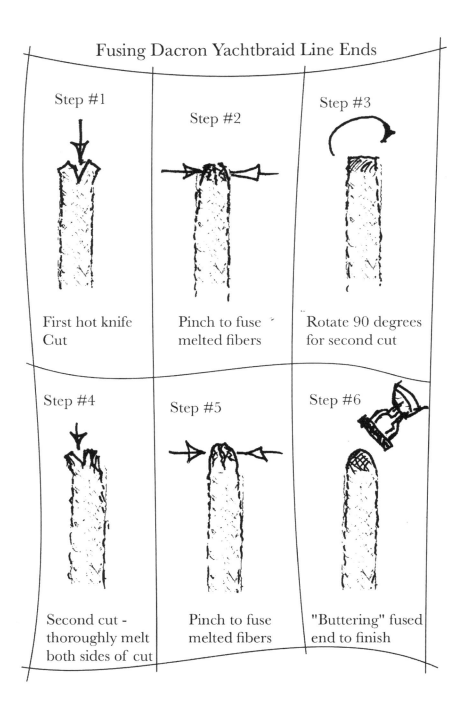

Step #1

First hot knife
Cut

Step #2

Pinch to fuse
melted fibers

Step #3

Rotate 90 degrees
for second cut

Step #4

Second cut -
thoroughly melt
both sides of cut

Step #5

Pinch to fuse
melted fibers

Step #6

"Buttering" fused
end to finish

With a regular straight hot knife cut, there is usually only a thin layer of fused material at the very end where it was melted and "buttered' with the hot knife or melted in a handy flame. The fused layer is rather thin and can be fractured easily from weathering or even from being stepped on. Then the end begins fraying into awkward clumps.

Begin by cutting into the end of the line, working the hot knife back and forth a bit to melt lots of fiber, and then fusing the mass by pressing it together while it is still molten. Cutting to the depth of one diameter (3/8" deep for 3/8" diameter line) is suggested. Making a second end cut at 90 degrees to the first, and then refusing that cut while molten, creates the solid fused rope end. The tip is then finished off with some hot knife buttering to smooth the solid fused mass.

Whipping the line is not required but is frequently done just to give things a finished seamanlike look.

[7.05] Finishing Line Fibers that Don't Fuse

2.   1.   3.

Many of the modern ultra-low-stretch fibers like Spectra and Vectran do not fuse well, even though most line made from those fibers has a Dacron cover. Sailmaker Chris Gillium showed me the following three ways to finish such line ends cleanly and efficiently.

Method #1 is the easiest—"milking" a bit of the Dacron cover toward the end until the core is "buried" a few line diameters, after which it is a simple matter to whip the cover end, proceeding to fuse it and butter it neatly. Even without sewing the core to the cover (which reduces "creep" as the cover stretches and the core doesn't) this is a good permanent solution, for even after a few season's use the core is still within an inch or two of the line's end causing no loss of utility.

Method #2 is just a bit more involved but provides a beautifully finished end that requires no whipping. The first step is to pull a few inches of core out from the cover and cut it off. The second is to carefully heat-fuse the edge of the cover "tube" so that it may be tucked inside itself. Chris tucks the core into a splicing fid's hollow end so he can neatly cut and fuse the cover with his hot knife without damaging the core.

In his most elegant version of this finishing #2, Chris sews the shortened core end to the fused cover edge, and then "milks" the cover toward the bitter end, which pulls the sewed edge into the core's interior, leaving the finished end seen in photo #2. A simpler version of this technique is to forgo the core-to-cover sewing step, simply working the cover end into the void from the removed core. This simpler approach benefits from a whipping to keep the inverted cover inside itself.

Method #3 is the solution for any line end that must be reeved through sheet stoppers or into an internal spar fitting, like a halyard on the mast or a mainsail outhaul on the boom. To form the reeving loop shown, a length of the core is first extracted, and then a length of the hollow cover is fed back through itself to form the reeving loop (shown here with a zip tie attached for easy reeving through sheet stoppers). The core and cover loop are then sewn together and whipped for a neat and functional long-lasting line end with reeving loop.

[7.06] Why Knot?

There is one little discussed factor that contributes greatly to successful sailboat racing and that is crew spirit and unity—successful racing is measured not only by finishing place but also by level of personal satisfaction and desire to do it again. The crew who've sailed many seasons together know this well but there are so many others who've searched and not yet found the team of boat, skipper, and ship mates to settle in with. Many skippers still search in vain for their permanent regular crew.

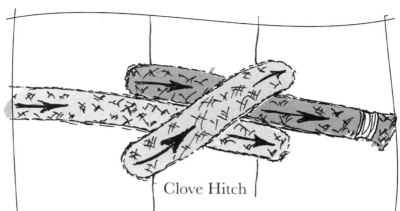

Clove Hitch

The Clove Hitch is easy to tie, easy to adjust,
and easy to untie. One thing to remember:
Important Note: This knot can slip out under
intermitent strains, like a tied up dinghy, if there
is no stopper knot in the rope's end.

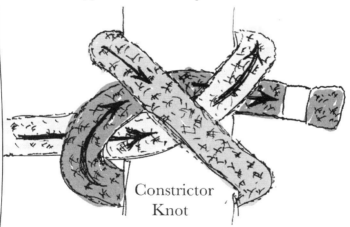

Constrictor Knot

The Constrictor Knot will not slip, and when
tied with three strand line is very difficult to untie.
Called a Thief's Knot by some, it was used as a
Tamperproof tie for grain sacks. Study the knot
and you will see it is a clove hitch with a twist.

Two Close Cousins--The Clove and The Constrictor

In yacht racing, as well as in my professional life, I would regularly find myself with a brand new team and a task at hand to accomplish. Effective teamwork relies on effective communication, and effective communication is generally more difficult with strangers.

A technique I sometime use is to involve a few of my team in learning to tie a useful new knot. There is something about the sharing of knowledge that fosters group unity. For me to teach you something useful is a gift, and for you to then pass this gift on to others makes us a community which improves our potential to communicate.

Understand how different it is to teach and learn a new knot than it is to lecture or be lectured about some way to do something. Try to make communication on your boat more like learning than lecturing. Building the team you want is the best alternative to finding it ready made.

These are two of my favorite knots to share, so maybe you can get a chance to learn them. I've drawn them here for fun with my shaky hand but you can find excellent illustrations and demonstrations online.

The first is the Zeppelin Hitch used to join two line ends together. This is a wonderful knot because it is strong and secure yet easy to untie once the load is removed—it does not jam! A most useful second feature is that it is still effective when the two line ends are of different diameters or types.

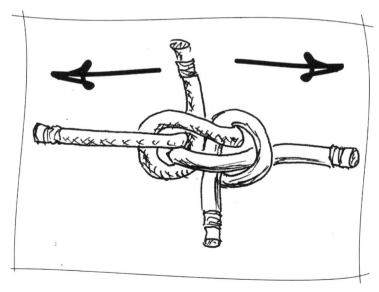

The Zeppelin Hitch

The second fine knot is the rolling hitch which is used to attach a line onto the middle of another line or spar—an invaluable knot to take the genoa sheet load from a winch override. This hitch can be quickly tied and has the marvelous virtue of holding securely in one direction while it can also slip easily in the opposite direction. Until modern "ascenders" were invented, a pair of stirrups each tied with its own rolling hitch made climbing up a taught vertical rope an easy matter.

So go learn how to tie a new knot or two and then teach it to others. Be a teacher and a "learning leader" to make this type of sharing a building block of your team's spirit and unity.

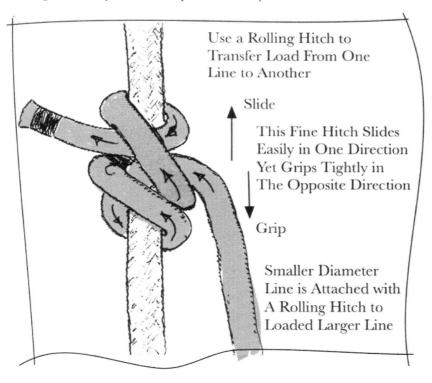

Use a Rolling Hitch to Transfer Load From One Line to Another

Slide

This Fine Hitch Slides Easily in One Direction Yet Grips Tightly in The Opposite Direction

Grip

Smaller Diameter Line is Attached with A Rolling Hitch to Loaded Larger Line

The Rolling Hitch

Use this fine hitch to attach your anchor's chafing strap or adjust your boat's fenders.

[7.07] Unsticking the Stuck: A Ritual of Boating

"Heat it up and bang it loose" is the age old solution to unsticking fasteners and fittings that are welded together with corrosion.

Torching to cause uneven thermal expansion of dissimilar metals is a frequently effective method, employed after the application of solvents such as Liquid Wrench have failed.   However heat application can damage painted surfaces and other material finishes.

Professional rigger Stan Harris offers an effective alternative he frequently uses to free up "turning bits" while hanging from his bosun's chair from various mastheads.   "Freeze Spray" is the generic term for aerosol cans of Tetrafluoroethane, a rapidly evaporating chemical whose "heat of vaporization" will quickly chill any surface it contacts.   The physics here are: Heat is required to boil the liquid Tetrafluoroethane into a gas so squirting the liquid onto a stuck bolt takes heat away from that bolt, which causes it to shrink a bit.

Stan fashions an insulating donut of foam to concentrate the chilling effect on the bolt or pin he wants to extract before applying Freeze Spray. Like the expansion forces created from applied heat, the shrinking forces of applied cooling cause different materials to move a bit in relationship to one another, which can help break the bonds of corrosion.

So consider arming your toolbox with this valuable tool so the next time you can't get it loose——"Chill it out to get it free".

[7.08] Anchoring: A Learning Process

The warm waters of anchorages in Mexico provided the school where I studied advanced anchoring. I developed the routine of donning mask, fins, and snorkel to inspect my anchor after setting it and squaring away the boat. This was such a rewarding pursuit that I advise all to make it part of their routine whenever possible.

The first concern was the holding ground and how well my anchor was set.   Then came an underwater survey to scout out important information like underwater obstacles that might hinder anchoring or exit from the anchorage should there be a weather change.

Next came an evaluation of adjacent boats' anchors, and that is where you obtain an education. Sometimes you will see an anchor lying on the bottom with a pile of chain on top and it is easy to picture that skipper's anchoring technique.   Sometimes you will see several boat lengths of chain laid out on the bottom from a plow type anchor that is lying on its side, never having penetrated a hard sand bottom.   Sometimes you'd encounter lightweight Danforth-type anchors with a tenuous hook to a rock that would be quickly dislodged by a shift in wind direction.

Each picture you see during these surveys adds to your ability to visualize what is happening to your ground tackle as you deploy it. Anchoring expertise involves the ability to visualize a three-dimensional model where the surface features are plotted and the underwater features projected. Accurate visualization combined with some intelligent analysis will produce expert anchoring skills.

Imagine having the vision of a keel-mounted underwater camera that could scan the terrain as you entered the anchorage for your initial survey, then project that information on the detailed mental chart you are drawing. Let us make a checklist of the useful information we would want to gather and how would we use it.

1. We want to know the depths and features of the bottom so that we can pick good holding ground and predict how much scope will be required. Modern graphic depth-sounder/fish-finders can provide much of this information.   Earlier chart study combined with actual observations can paint the topsides features.

2. The layout of the anchorage can now be evaluated as to which parts offer protection from which directions of wind and waves. Adding in any boats that are already anchored and factoring in your deductions about the scope of each, you can visualize the swinging circles of each of your future neighbors to see how your boat will fit into this new neighborhood.

3. Anchorages with less protection from the open water outside are frequently populated with boats anchored bow and stern so they are always pointed into the swell. Vessels with bow and stern anchors should be immediately identified because they will remain stationary and can become obstacles to any boat swinging nearby on a single hook.

4. Likewise allow for different boat types to react differently to changing conditions.   One classic demonstration of this principle in action is the well known "La Paz Waltz" where tidal current and wind direction reverse periodically.

Imagine fifty to sixty boats of all different types neatly streaming back from their single hooks pointed into wind and current in a beautiful city side harbor. Now reverse the wind and watch the lightweight multihulls spin around and back into the sterns of the lower freeboard sailboats that have been held more or less in place by the tidal current acting on their keels and rudders. Add in some sport fishers, cabin cruisers, *pangas*, and now reverse the tide as the wind clocks and builds, pushing each type of boat in a different manner to its new attitude.

There is nothing orderly about this waltz. It's more of a disorderly rave with each participant doing their own thing.   Keeping this choreography in mind, evaluate your new neighborhood accordingly.

5. Having picked your spot, noted the depth, and calculated your scope and swing radius, you "go fishing" to hook your anchor into the earth. That term, "hook into the earth" provides a guiding image for me as I imagine letting out rode with the boat slowly backing, these actions synchronized so that the anchor touches bottom a few feet before reaching its final spot. As the anchor grazes the bottom and rode is payed out, the fluke begins to dig in. If the backing speed exceeds the pay out rate, the anchor will be dragged before it can start digging in. If

the pay out rate exceeds the back down rate, the chain will fall in piles or loops making the final backing down to set the anchor process much less precise.

6. Setting the hook is a most important step. It involves balancing the forces of back down thrust with scope and bottom holding characteristics to dig the anchor in without breaking it loose. Too short a scope and the anchor breaks out while too much scope reduces the digging force and it does not bury properly. With proper scope (3:1 is good for plow anchors because they need lots of pull to bury and 4:1 or more for lighter weight faster digging anchors), backing down at more than half throttle for a minute or two should deliver a solid set.

7. The last step is to let out additional scope for optimal holding power and set the chafing strap or snubber. Then slip into your mask and fins to look around and see how accurate and successful your visualization was.

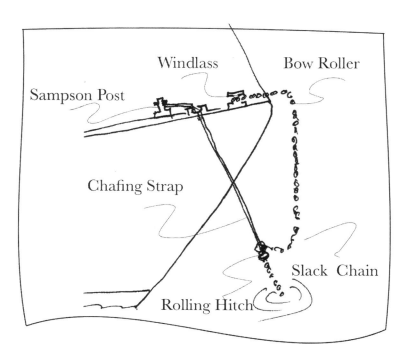

Chafing Strap or Anchor Rode "Snubber"

[7.09] Using a Gear-Saving "Chafing Strap"

Not every sailor does much anchoring so here is something I worked out that gave me piece of mind in my years of living "off the grid and on the hook."

Centuries ago, when sailing ships were anchored with great hemp hawsers so large a man's arms could not encircle them, a "chafing strap" was used to secure the hawser to the ship.

Not to be confused with a rash-producing athletic undergarment, this strap was made of stout braided line and was secured to the giant hemp hawser with a version of the modern rolling hitch. The other end was secured to the mooring bit with another hitch. The chafing strap was an essential component to protect an irreplaceable great hawser.

Modern sailors should continue this practice to protect their valuable anchor rode—for no one wants to live with a chafe repair in the middle of a long piece of expensive line. An elastic chafing strap/snubber system for anchoring today will protect expensive anchor windlasses and bow rollers from the huge shock loads that can develop when rough water invades a windy anchorage.

[7.10] Square Drive Fasteners

My grandfather drove Chevrolets so my father usually had a Chevy. My father was an early convert to Phillips head screws so I've been a Phillips man myself—up until square drive Robertson heads came into my life. It all started with using my "Pocket Hole" jig (this is the gizmo that facilitates drilling those angled countersunk holes for screwing wood pieces edge to end while making cabinet faces) and the square drive screws supplied with the jig.

Then, as with true love, my affection expanded to other dimensions of my love object.

Removing corroded, stripped Phillips heads is a penance frequently paid for buggering-up the heads during installation, especially with self-tapping screws. Corrosion is accelerated if the head was deformed during installation.

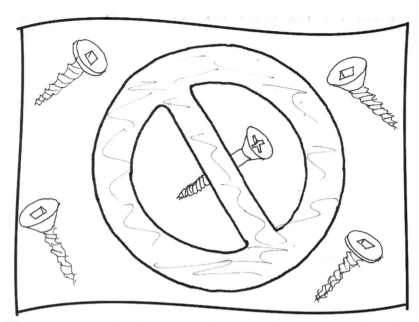

There are two main factors contributing to deformation of heads in 316 stainless Phillips screws. One factor is that 316 stainless is manufactured relatively soft so threads can be cut in the screw manufacturing process, and 316 is not easily hardened after manufacture like the steel screws commonly used in building and household projects. We can see how hard these construction screws (commonly called "drywall screws") are by how quickly they wear out driver bits, which have in turn been hardened so they don't wear so quickly. Adding to the potential damage of a hardened tool driving a softer fastener is the turning resistance of un-lubricated threads cutting into hard fiberglass or aluminum; this factor is easily reduced with a bit of cutting wax.

Another problem is the tapered fit of Mr. Phillips' head design quickly disengages with reduced inward driving pressure. This is an intentional design feature from before we had adjustable torque power drivers—the head is intended to limit over-driving. The driver "cams out" of the Phillips screw head under increased load, which unintentionally occurs when working in awkward positions. The driver's cam out initiates the buggering-up process.

Once you've tried square drive heads its unlikely you'll go back to Phillips.

The increased contact surface of the inserted square driver distributes the load over a larger area, putting less pressure on the soft 316 stainless which reduces the chance of damage under difficult driving conditions. Little inward pressure is required to maintain full contact between driver and fastener. A most wonderful side effect of the square drive is the one-handed driving ease you get from the way a fastener pushed onto the driver remains in place. This is a great feature if you're swinging from a bosun's chair or working where you need that second hand to hold something else.

Although it has been decades since I used silicon slot head bronze screws in wooden boats I can now see how superior square drive heads would have been.

The last surprise is how effective the proper sized square driver is for removing corroded and buggered-up Phillips head fasteners This capability converted me completely when the inserted square driver easily backed out the buggered Phillips head screw.

[7.11] Trio of Tools

Here are three little-known tools that are most useful aboard a boat.

"A" is a German pair of "force multiplying parallel jaw" pliers made by Kinpex, most interesting because there are three moving parts—the two handles and the jaw part that remains parallel to the fixed jaw as it slides—like the adjustable jaw wrench.

The design of this tool provides excellent gripping force with minimal chance of marring the flat-sided object gripped. The moving jaw is actuated by the protrusion from the pivoting handle part with considerable mechanical advantage. You can calculate the advantage by measuring the lever arm ratio—the distance from the fulcrum (the pivot pin in this case) to the point where force is applied—in this tool it is better than 10:1, which is more than twice the grip ratio of regular pliers.

"B" is a "long reach compound needle nose plier" available online if not in your local store. This tool solves the problem of applying a firm grip in a limited access situation. A grip ratio of 3:1 obtained 5 inches away from a 1-1/2 inch diameter hole means you can get at hard to reach objects with far more gripping strength than alternative tweezer type tools. If you study the drawing a bit, you will see four moving parts, which makes this tool like a needle nose plier that has another plier attached where the handles would be.

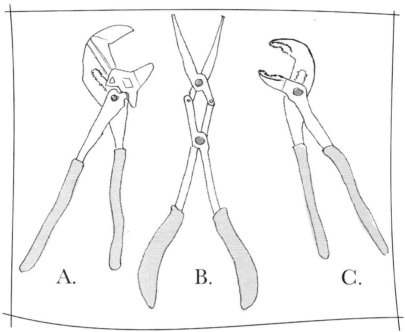

"C" looks like a normal "Channel Lock" plier, yet it has two distinct differences. The first feature you notice is that the fulcrum pivot point adjustment of this tool has 12 notches compared to the 5 to 8 positions in channel types. More fulcrum positions translate into more options to adjust the handles to the best distance for your hand to apply a powerful grip. (A similar wide range of adjustment is provided in the Kinpex design.) The second feature is the design of the jaws which provide excellent gripping of different shapes and sizes of objects from large hex nuts to small round pins and most everything in between. This tool is also made of a much harder steel than normally found, which provides sharper jaw teeth at the price of some increased brittleness.

Although your tool box increases in size and weight as you add specialty tools, I've found these three worth more than their cost of passage.

[7.12] Document Your Boat's Systems

SERVICE NOTES & MANUALS

One Place For
All the Important Stuff

I mentioned the racer's notebook earlier and now I want to suggest that every skipper have his own folder of notes.

A boat can have many systems, each with its associated plumbing and wiring, which usually only need attention when something fails or malfunctions. Sorting out a complicated system during a period of stress (foul weather causes more failures than fair) should be made as easy as possible. Good documentation with appropriate notes and diagrams is most appreciated.

Additionally, if the documentation is too broad, as in having all the service, parts, and operational manuals on an encyclopedic shelf, there can be too much to sort through. A binder with clear notes, copies of manual pages where needed, and with diagrams labeled to match the labels on the plumbing and wiring blocks will be a valuable resource should someone unfamiliar with the boat have to trouble-shoot or repair

[7.13] *Spinnaker Poles on a Cruising Sailboat*

There were many "Sidewalk Supervisors" monitoring my progress loading up at the yacht club guest dock for my third trip down to Mexico, so there was no shortage of advice and editorial comments about various choices I had made.

"Two spinnaker poles on a cruising boat?   With my cruising asymmetrical chute I don't even need one," noted one expert.

"Seems like a fish with a pair of bicycles in his garage," said another.

I didn't bother answering those onlookers, but let me tell you my reasons for carrying a pair of poles.

1. A truly self-sufficient offshore cruiser would carry some sort of spare spar to jury rig as a replacement for a broken boom. A spinnaker pole is a far better alternative than lashing oars and boat hooks together. Sometimes sailboats lose their masts and lack engine range or capability to get safely to port, in which case an extra spar or two for jury-rigging some sail power could make a huge difference in how their stories end.

2. When cruising offshore you sometimes have to "sail the wind that blows," making the best of whatever conditions you encounter once your passage begins. My first run down to Mexico on *Scallywag* found us in three days of substantial breeze on a broad reach down to Bahia Magdalena. This leg would have been far more difficult to manage without the pole to wing out a small part of the roller reefing genoa, using a simple trick I learned on my old Cal 27.

That trick was to use both a fore guy and an after guy to stabilize the pole between the opposing forces of topping lift, fore, and after guys. Many cruisers omit the after guy assuming the genoa sheet performs that function when the sail is set, not thinking so much about what happens during the transitions between jibes or other sail trim changes. Once the sheet is eased the pole is free to swing forward and then to swing back as far as the fore guy will allow—assuming the fore guy has been set.

With the pole stabilized by two guys, it was easy to adjust both sail area and clew position appropriately for the wind strength and point of sail without the pole swinging about. To make jibes easy with my end-for-end rigged pole, a second lazy after guy was rigged on the other side of the boat.

My single-handing jibe technique was to preset the lazy after guy, ease the fore guy just a bit, and adjust the autopilot to reach up ten degrees to help stabilize the boat. Tripping the pole from the mast under a bit of load was done carefully as the lazy jib sheet was placed in its jaws and the pole was thrust out to the opposite side. Presetting the new after guy kept the pole stable once the new mast end was made fast. Back in the cockpit I set the autopilot to steer through the jibe as I handled the sheets and swung the boom over, producing an easily controlled singlehanded jibe.

3. My stowage system for one pole (see photo) provided two great benefits. Attached at head height to the mast with the other end lashed into the sturdy bow pulpit it provided a stable and handy spar to hold when going forward to watch dolphins bow wave riding or for any other purpose. It also provided a bit of bowsprit through which the cruising spinnaker's tack line would lead, after first passing through the spare anchor roller. This forward tack lead provided a large enough slot that I could carry a genoa under the spinnaker in light wind close reaching, which was an awesome capability on a cruising boat.

Scallywag tied to "A" Dock in Marina Vallarta in 1991. Note that no other docks are yet complete making Scallywag *one of only two dozen boats in residence.*

4. I stowed my R.I.B. dinghy inverted on the foredeck, which provided a challenge for the single hander to launch and retrieve. Again, the pole provided an attachment point to rig the lifting halyard with an outhaul line run through the pole end fitting, to provide a straight up pull when raising the dinghy. Once the inverted dinghy was off the deck, it was easy to rotate the dinghy into an upright attitude by hooking the other spin halyard to the inside lifting bridle. With the outhaul line

around the lifting halyards, it was easy to swing the pole and dinghy outboard without it pushing toward the mast. Stowage was the reverse operation.

5. Effective flopper-stoppers of some sort can turn an open roadstead into a pleasant anchorage, and outrigging the stopper's lift ring away from the boat increases effectiveness of the unit by lengthening the lever arm to provide greater roll resistance. I carried two flopper-stoppers so I could rig one on each side of the boat with the two poles. *Scallywag's* double flopper-stopper rig frequently made for a comfortable and private anchorage that few other boats were prepared to share.

A penalty of finding comfort in rolling waters is that you are slower to notice conditions deteriorating and sometimes have to bail out in a hurry. Tripping the outboard end of the pole would allow the out-rigged flopper-stopper to return to the side of the boat, and a second lift line attached to a corner of the rectangular unit facilitated easy retrieval, even if the boat was now underway. Once a safe course through the swells and out of the roadstead had been set on the autopilot, the poles and flopper-stoppers could be properly stowed.

6. Poles out-rigged on both sides of the boat provided additional mooring points for the windsurfers so they wouldn't bang against the hull, and were handy for visiting hard dinghies with inadequate rub rails and fenders.

The moral is: Although bicycles for fish is a ridiculous proposition, extra spars on a cruising boat are well worth considering.

[7.14] *Handy Cockpit GPS Holder*

One part of the creative act is to see something in an alternate reality, like when Picasso mounted bicycle handlebars with a bicycle seat attached and a bull's head was created. To look around at what is at hand and to imagine how it can be fashioned to serve a different purpose is something sailors do.

Here is something I worked out to solve a recurrent need.

Immediate access to GPS information is very useful in the tactical management of a sailboat race, and as tactician I went through a lot of alternatives for keeping my portable handy. I put this device together to hold my handheld GPS when I move from boat to boat helping with tactics and mentoring new racers.

Cut the top off a clear plastic bottle, ballast with something heavy so it doesn't blow away, and you have a no-cost holder for your handheld GPS or VHF. Works fine for cell phones, iPods, handheld remotes, or what have you.

[7.15] *Cockpit Cover*

My Marina del Rey is a dirty place with airplane pollution, the collected material of all sorts that blows off the roofs of adjacent buildings (that's why your boat gets so dirty when it's windy), and everything else that falls out of our air. Boats get dirty and if you use them when they're dirty, you get dirty. Many marinas are not that much cleaner.

Washing the boat down and drying it off before use is rarely possible if you are a Wednesday night racer or tight scheduled weekender. Boat covers do keep the boat clean but are large and expensive, besides taking lots of storage space when not deployed.

We decided to save room, time, and money by covering only the back half of the boat, which also eliminated much fitting and fastener design.

"Who sits on the deck forward of the mast?" we asked ourselves.

As a venerable race boat, our vessel has lots of winches and each had its own expensive bonnet—things we would not need with a new cockpit cover. We opened a cold beverage and began to design and budget a simple solution that rendered many benefits: a clean cockpit when we get to the boat; no need for individual winch covers and the time to take them off, stow them, find them, and then put them back on; protection for the varnished wood work, and something that could be used for cockpit shade when needed.

To economize, we did a joint project with our friend Oliver the sailmaker. Gordon and I would do all the fitting work on the boat and Oliver could stay in the loft making money, which he likes to do. And a good deal for us because we did the messing about with boats which is what we like to do.

(Here is a good general boat project tip: save your professional's time futzing with you and your project in the field. Futz around by yourself or with your futzing crew and keep the professional's time focused on defining and accomplishing the task.)

An accurate pattern is an excellent construction document, for it is a definitive statement of shapes and dimensions when transferring the design from the boat to the shop, so we started cutting and taping a cheap tarp to make the initial pattern.

As some finish details are dependent on others, it can be useful to develop the pattern in stages, with one stage finished so that fitting can be done for the subsequent detailing.

Oliver took our tarp pattern, figured how material would be seamed, ordered the Sunbrella, and put together our cover to the first stage of construction. Back to the boat with lots of clamps and bits of bungee we secured the cover around its sides to the slotted toe rail. We determined the final shape by stapling a hem around the perimeter and then back to the shop for final cutting and sewing. One more trip to the boat to mark exact grommet locations and finishing details around the backstay.

A brief visit to the shop for grommets and we had it back to the boat for the final detail of locating the elk hide chafe protection patches at the wear points of winch and other hardware contact.

Since we were looking at the top side of the cover and the shop needed to locate the patches on the underside we needed to figure out an easy method of documenting the decisions on the underside surface. Our solution was pretty simple. We figured about where each patch should go along with its shape and size. We then cut the patches from the hide, punched three holes around the edge of each patch, and sewed them in place on the topside with a few simple stitches though the cover, It was then an easy job for the seamstress to mark the underside location by feeling the patch on the topside.

Breaking the project into stages made the job easy and efficient for the pros. We saved some bucks and got exactly the cover we wanted.

The women on the race crew were especially grateful going to the club not having sacrificed their clean bottoms to wipe the LA fallout off the boat.

[7.16] Another Case of Operator Error

(Or maybe inadequate instruction)

In 1996 I wanted to see how much had changed at Nuevo Vallarta, Mexico, since my engine failure five years before, but the Marina entrance was still the same obstacle course with underwater sandbars. Designed like several other Mexican marina entrance channels, one side was a straight jetty and the other side a jagged saw-tooth array of small rock jetties set perpendicular to the channel at about seventy-five foot intervals, each with shallow beaches built up behind.

An engineer once explained the concept to me. The shallow beaches and jetties on the saw-tooth side were designed to absorb and dissipate wave energy from swells entering the channel, reducing the uncomfortable surge inside the marina.

Not very effective at dampening wave energy, this design also helps generate bumps and gullies in the channel floor—bumps that greatly reduce the entrance depth when bump, boat, and wave trough share the same time and space. *Scallywag*'s rudder reminded me of this fact when I sailed in to visit the just-opened Paradise Village Resort and Marina one afternoon at high tide.

I had checked in with the marina Dock Master by radio before entering and was assured there was no problem with entrance depth, and a friend with a house in the area had drawn me a chart of the bottom contour. I felt confident *Scallywag*'s five foot-draft and the high tide would give us plenty of margin from the eight-foot minimum depth reported at low tide.

Despite following the charted channel perfectly, *Scallywag* shuddered frightfully as she encountered the first big bump while floating deeply in the trough of a three foot swell. I could feel the shock through the steering wheel, and my heart sank as the spade rudder hit bottom twice more.

The rudder damage was immediately obvious when the rudder jammed at about ten degrees of turn to starboard and maximum force was required on the wheel to unjam it and turn to port. With the handheld VHF radio I again contacted the Dock Master to explain my dilemma and request one of the dozen slips that had been built. As all the slips were along one dock to our left, I planned my approach as a large circle to port, the direction the rudder would move. The Dock Master was there to catch our "spring line" as we eased up to the dock.

My next move after getting fenders deployed and mooring lines secured was to don swimming suit, fins, mask, and snorkel to see how bad things were. Even with the poor visibility in this muddy estuary it was clear the rudder shaft was bent and I could see white shredded fiberglass where the top trailing tip of the rudder must have snapped off as it was wedged against the hull. I surfaced and called for a hack saw and a turn of the steering wheel to locate a cut line that would permit full articulation of the bent rudder.

With a full range of rudder angulation restored it was time for a dock hose shower and a cold beer. As it happened, the trauma was so severe *Scallywag* and I needed a full five days to recover at this nearly empty and newly opened deluxe resort before returning to the boatyard in Marina Vallarta for haul out and repair.

However there was another dramatic entrance-channel grounding on the third day of our recovery, and that is the tale I will tell.

Recompense was an an Ericson 32 sailboat that had departed Nuevo Vallarta for a trip back to the U.S. on the day before our grounding. They had been driven back by a rare winter storm and I recognized the boat and crew as they approached the entrance. The storm surge had generated a few breaking waves in the channel and it was clear this would be a far worse situation than *Scallywag* had encountered three days before. Repeated radio hails failed to get a response from *Recompense* so I jumped into the dinghy and motored full speed to warn them.

I was too late, for by the time I reached them they had already bounced several times off the bottom and the rig had loosened so much that the mast was now tracing circles in the sky as it wobbled drunkenly about. Deformation of the hull was the only probable cause for the loose rig and major structural damage was the only probable cause for the hull deformation.

This was obviously a very ugly situation!

It was certain my six horsepower outboard could render negligible towing assistance, so I requested they deploy their bow anchor and rode to my dinghy so a kedge could be anchored further up the channel with which they could winch themselves free. Alas, they had secured the bow anchor for their trip north with multiple wraps of an old jib sheet and lots of knots ("If you can't tie good knots, tie lots of bad ones" is common advice) and they were still fumbling about when two pangas with their powerful outboard engines arrived and passed them a line.

I scurried out of the way and listened to the sickening sound as the keel hit bottom again and again—the rig getting looser with every bump. The next chapter of this story would involve two-part underwater epoxy and scuba gear, I thought, all of which I gathered.

My neighbor boat was owned by a retired Canadian heart surgeon named John and his wife Sandy, an accomplished sailing couple I'd known for a few years by now. John was recruited to be my dinghy operator and epoxy mixer, and a pair of mixing boards with two large putty knives were placed in the dinghy alongside a one gallon kit of Splash Zone underwater epoxy from *Scallywag*'s emergency repair kit.

One more radio call to *Recompense* got the response that they were now secure in a slip across the channel in the decrepit Nuevo Vallarta Marina and all was well. I unzipped my dive suit, but kept everything in readiness in case things were not as secure as reported—which turned out to be the case.

Next we heard a radio request for extra bilge pumps and I figured John and I would soon be called to duty.

"John, you'll be in the dinghy mixing batches of the putty for me to apply. You hand me the new loaded mixing board when I finish applying the one at hand."

"How should I mix it?" he inquired.

"Mix it real well." I responded.

Gathering up a couple of underwater dive lights to help visibility—as the winter sun was starting to set—we loaded up and motored across to the stricken vessel. Quite a crowd had assembled on the dock to render advice and I dove down with a light to survey the damage. Severe it was, with a gaping smile-shaped crack open at the leading edge of the keel where it met the hull. Visible cracks could be seen all around the keel and there was one bad rip which opened from the keel up the port side, under the head area of the boat. This was an area with extensive interior details molded to strengthen the boat around the mast and keel loads.

No wonder the rig went slack, I said to myself. The bulkhead on the port side must surely be crushed, requiring complete demolition of the interior to access that section of the hull and keel stump. I surfaced and asked John to start mixing Splash Zone, and to report the extent of the damage to *Recompense*'s unhappy owner.

Underwater loading a spreader full of goo from the mixing board and pushing it into the gaping hole was a surprisingly difficult and messy process. Stringy filaments would suspend themselves in the water and then wrap around whatever they encountered whether it be part of me or my scuba gear. Soon I noticed my epoxy-coated gloved hands were contaminating my mouthpiece when I surfaced to instruct John to mix smaller batches and to push the mass close to one corner of the mixing board for more effective application.

I must have been working a long time, for daylight was completely gone when I was notified the leak had diminished enough that one small pump was keeping up with the inflow. I was taking a last dive to smooth things out a bit and work some more putty into the biggest cracks, when John reached down and tapped my shoulder, signaling me to surface and communicate.

"How much more putty will you need?" he asked.

I replied, "Not much. Why do you ask? Are we running out?"

"No, I just wanted to know if I should open the other can," said John.

Nearly swallowing my goo-coated regulator from laughter, I contemplated how much more effective would have been a dozen kids

chewing up packages of gum and handing them down—not to mention how much cheaper than the several hundred dollars a one gallon kit of Splash Zone costs.

The bright side of John's mixing error is that the Part "A" material that was stuck all over my dive suit and gear was ever so much easier to remove as soft goo than if it was hardened epoxy.

A benefit of the experience was improvement in my plans for the next emergency underwater repair job. In retrospect, the right response would be to have a few tubes of silicone caulk/adhesive along with a caulking gun to apply it for a temporary fix. Application would have been exponentially easier with a caulking gun, and *Recompense's* structure was far too compromised for any epoxy putty to do any good. Having mixed epoxy putty in a caulking tube with a gun to apply it could be a most effective repair for less extensive damage.

My next trip stateside, I picked up a dozen empty caulking tubes, a few of which stayed in my emergency supplies to be loaded with epoxy when needed and the rest were distributed to friends after being told this story.

"So where was you when the brains was passed out?"

"Outside, a peein' on me foot."

The sailors with the most time get the best weather.

The lovely thing about cruising is

that planning usually turns out to be of little use.

The sail, the play of its pulse so like our own lives: so thin and yet so full of life, so noiseless when it labors hardest, so noisy and impatient when least effective.

8. ENDNOTE - PASSING IT ALONG

[8.01] Becoming a "Waterman"

One great joy of my decade sailing around the West Coast of Mexico was learning to live as a "Waterman." I thought this a wonderfully descriptive word for one who lives in close contact, and sings close harmony with the aquatic world.

Before that decade I'd learned to sail, efficiently harnessing the forces of wind and water, sometimes in competition with others and sometimes alone just for the satisfaction of doing it well. And as a preteen I'd followed my interest in underwater swimming to become certified as a SCUBA diver. But it was not until I became a full-time live aboard, sailing around the isolated anchorages in these warm waters, that I discovered the option of living as a Waterman.

A good friend once said of Mexico's Sea of Cortez, "It's full of beautiful scenery, some of which is above water."

Discovering the beauty and variety of that underwater world became my key to the Waterman's club—an informal fellowship where the members somehow recognize each other and signal that recognition with some shared understanding of the universe around them.

Summer in the Sea of Cortez includes lots of hot weather, staying out of the sun at mid-day, wearing little if any clothing, and spending many hours a day in the refreshing hospitality of the underwater world. As one might do when camping in a mountain wilderness using most every opportunity to hike around in the refreshing feast of nature, snorkeling was a central feature of each day. It was not unusual to head off for an hours-long underwater hike, sometimes taking a spear gun to accompany the knife that was usually strapped to my leg when I swam (I have a powerful appetite for fresh scallops which I eat while treading water, diving down for the next one as soon as my mouth is empty enough to replace my snorkel).

After anchoring in some snug cove at an uninhabited island, the next move was usually to grab mask, fins, and snorkel to dive the anchor — which means to inspect and assess the security I could expect from the anchor's grip to the earth should weather conditions suddenly change. The contours and features of the bottom, along with the type and consistency of the material found on that floor could have a huge impact on how a different wind would change my situation.

A secure hook into the earth below, no underwater hazards close at hand, a safe escape route planned and mentally charted—these were the elements of a good neighborhood. Sometimes these good neighborhoods came with a handy cafeteria with a delicious variety of the freshest seafood.

There was a moment that knew that I'd become a Waterman. After a couple of weeks up in my Santa Monica home, looking in on my mother in her assisted-living apartment, I drove back down the peninsula to Puerto Escondido where my venerable 37-foot sloop was anchored at the edge of this popular "hurricane hole." A call on the handheld VHF radio produced a ride from the dinghy dock out to my *Scallywag* floating serenely in this scenic caldera. After first deploying the sunshade and shedding my sweat-soaked clothing, I strapped on my knife, grabbed snorkel, mask, and fins, and slipped into the water swimming naked to the nearby rocky shore where I enjoyed lunch at the "Raw Bar" forty yards from my home. Looking like smiles when mostly buried, "pen scallops" (*callos de hache* in Spanish) peek from the sand and frisbee-sized rock scallops adjacent for the taking—and take them I did.

I had become 100% naked Waterman—one of the most satisfying transformations of my life!

Cruising, I learned how little I needed, not how much

If one does not know to which port one is sailing, no wind is favorable

[8.02] Self Confidence —Taming the "Willies"

The further a sailboat ventures from shore the smaller it seems to be. Likewise, the more the weather deteriorates, the more fragile the hull and rig seem to be. There are many vulnerabilities one must accept when sailing offshore.

Many perils, like hitting a nearly-submerged shipping container while sailing at six knots during the dark of night, are potentially fatal— preventable only by effective action after the fact rather than by any action to forestall that event. Somehow the offshore sailor must make good preparations with a "bail out bag," life raft, and other emergency survival gear, and rest assured they can be efficiently deployed and utilized should they ever be required.

Most offshore-racing sailors have been presented with weather challenges and gear failures which were easily mastered with crew experience and boat preparedness. Having experienced a powerful downdraft that knocked our race boat nearly flat and blew out the spinnaker I was much better prepared when the same thing happened to me while solo sailing across the Sea of Cortez.

Sailboat handling characteristics change dramatically as wind and sea state increase, and it is only through experience with those conditions that comfort comes. But before comfort arrives, skills must be built and tested. Confidence in tested skills helps banish the "willies."

What are these willies of which I speak? They are the unnamed fears. They are the fears of perils too numerous to count. They are the self doubts that you will not be able to perform in the face of potential challenge.

Sailing in unfamiliar waters, whether they be at sea or ashore, alerts our danger reflexes and raises our guard level. I'm reminded of snow skiing where speed and a relaxed ability to adjust to terrain make for exhilarating fun, but when mixed with too much fear of the degree of slope or unfamiliar terrain the body stiffens and the skills disappear. With greater experience and higher skill level comes confidence in more challenging circumstances, and defanging the willies involves much the same process.

Lastly, I'll mention that experience at sea in a sailboat helps the spirit harmonize with nature in a special way—and that is the music that drowns out the willies.

[8.03] Fatal Events

I wrote this two days after the 37-foot yacht *Aegean* was destroyed during the famous international Newport to Ensenada Sailboat Race.

Three of the four crew's bodies were recovered and the fourth was presumed lost after extensive search efforts were complete. My sincerest sympathies go out to all who've suffered and all who will suffer from this tragic loss of life at sea. Such losses have touched my life, and I know how profound they can be.

As with the classic Greek tragedies, we humans seek an understanding that will make sense out of the great suffering we witness. "Why did this happen? What can I learn to prevent it from happening to me and mine?"

Having considerable experience racing and sailing off-shore, I can imagine all sorts of possible explanations for how an experienced sailor with his crew of three friends came to be run down. It's easy to imagine the scope of destruction as a vessel with hundreds or thousands of times the mass of its fragile target shatters the fiberglass shell with the impact, and chews up the pieces in turbulence and prop wash. But even with the larger vessel taking less than three minutes to travel a mile, there would still have been plenty of opportunity for the tiny sailboat to determine the collision course (the night was clear with several miles of visibility) and take evasive action.

My first reaction is to place the blame on some lapse of seamanship —not because of some special inside knowledge about the event, but because I want to think that this fate can be avoided with greater education and vigilance. I want to feel sure that I would never be run down (although I nearly have been!) because I know better and I'm more careful.

Good seamanship and keeping a proper watch should insure that no one ever suffers such a fate, and my imagination will seek explanations that blame lapses of seamanship and watch-keeping for this tragedy. As in the tragic plots of classic Greek drama, I seek to discover the *hamartia,*, or "tragic mistake," that kept the heroes of the *Aegean* from recognizing their approaching fate and devising counter measures.

What mistake caused this tragedy, and whose mistake was it?

If the three recovered bodies were not dressed in their on-watch clothing, we could deduce that there was only one sailor on watch with the others engaged below. The winds were so light when *Aegean*'s location signal was lost at 1:30 am that the boat was drifting more than sailing, and rolling up the slatting genoa foresail while waiting for wind to return is an acceptable option in such conditions for a Cruising Class racer.

It is terribly easy for a solitary on-deck watch to get lulled asleep on a quiet night with nothing to do—except *keep watch*!

Or perhaps the deck watch was alert and was tracking the approaching vessel, but misjudged its speed. Perhaps the battery banks had been so depleted during the previous fifteen hours of sailing (with refrigerator, instruments, radios, and night lighting a steady drain) that the engine wouldn't start when called on at the last minute to propel the *Aegean*'s escape. With no powerful signaling device at hand, the crew could not effectively alert the approaching ship.

Or perhaps two men on watch were so focused on trimming their slatting sails and turning their unresponsive helm in the frustratingly faint breeze that came and went during that part of their race. Perhaps they were not aware of their approaching doom until it was too late to react.

So some responsibility always falls on the poor victims, not because they are guilty, but because we want to be certain that such a fate is not in store for us. We are different—so we will be safe, we assure ourselves. We recognize that *hamartia*, and we will not repeat it.

A few days later the Aegean's GPS track, recorded with a smart phone app, was published and the truth was revealed. The boat had tragically motored in an arrow-straight line for several hours in wind too light for them to sail effectively. Their course was direct to the northern tip of Isla Coronado del Norte where debris from the boat was later recovered.

Evidence pointed to a single watch-keeper in the cockpit and three asleep below with the boat motoring unsupervised under autopilot on a fatal course—a course that none on board were alert to alter before the fatal collision of fragile boat against surf-washed rocks in the middle of the night.

Dead reckoning?
Dead without it.

The sea finds out everything you did wrong

[8.04] Be the Safety Guy

This message has been saved for the end because it is most important and I want it to stick with you and spread to others.

I've been around a wide variety of boating accidents and experienced a great many more through my participation as a radio communicator and hearing first hand the stories of others. One thing they have in common is how they either benefited from the presence of a "safety guy" (of any gender) onboard—or suffered from the absence. The safety guy, sometimes the safety committee, is a most important position. Please make sure that position doesn't go vacant.

The "safety guy attitude" keeps safety issues in focus during planning and execution of all boating activity, even if being the lifeguard is not part of the job description.

When stepping aboard as a new crew; whether it be a race, a cruise, or just a daysail, take a look around the boat to locate things like fire extinguishers, first aid kit, PFD's, and VHF radio. This is a proper activity that impresses the knowledgable skipper that you are a valuable crew.

When some inexperienced hand is performing an assignment, you'd keep an eye out. Sometimes it is easy to see if another crew fully understands the import of the activity of something like hoisting the spinnaker halyard. It would take careful instruction to ensure a first timer was prepared as the halyard transitions quickly from a lightly loaded line to a very heavily loaded one when the sail fills with wind. If that halyard is not wrapped around a winch or lead through a closed stopper, that crew could be lifted from the deck, suffer severe rope burns, or both.

A race boat heading toward the finish line in a crowded harbor with other competitors close at hand might find its crew's attention focused on sail trim and tactical concerns with less attention to surrounding traffic. You can be the safety guy with the hand bearing compass to monitor the bearing of the approaching tanker.

"If the bearing remains constant as we approach, then we are on an intersecting course," you can say, explaining the compass' use.

The safety guy proudly accepts safety as a primary component of seamanship, as I hope you all do.

ABOUT THE AUTHOR

Tim Tunks—Satisfied Sailor

The author is an interesting guy who combined a variety of life experiences with a love of sailing, a combination that has illuminated his thoughts and actions for many decades.

Leaving the Ivy League enclave of high school in suburban New Jersey for the University of California at Santa Barbara Engineering School, Tim Tunks discovered the Sixties, a decade that delivered enduring values and philosophies. Graduating with a degree in theater, he continued through graduate school, professional apprenticeships, and into a university teaching career—a career that then segued into professional entertainment design and production in Las Vegas.

It was on Lake Mead that Tim fell in love with sailing, ignorantly buying his first awkward sailboat, and reading sailing books voraciously. That period was most important because this discovery of sailing was reinforced by his professional life. Both required analytical visualization of what was to happen and a detailed notion of the various forces and elements at play. To produce the event visualized, these elements and forces had to be sorted and managed.

For Tim, learning to sail combined the vector analysis learned during his engineering studies and the ability to multi-task in executing a complex event—a skill that stage production required. (He says he still "sees" the vector arrows that measure the forces at play as sails are trimmed and the boat is steered through the waves.)

As yacht racing became an important part of Tim's seamanship development, his theater and education communication techniques proved useful and productive to bond effective teams that also forged life-long friendships.

The decades of theatrical design ended as the lucky decade of cruising by sail in the welcoming Pacific waters of Mexico began. *Scallywag*, a venerable 37-foot Bruce King-designed tall-rigged racer/cruiser of the CCA class became his home. It was a decade of living off the grid, frequently sailing solo to spend time in isolated anchorages where the Ham radio provided the social life and nature provided the entertainment. It was during this period that Tim picked up the moniker of "Padretimo," a title bestowed with some irony because of his propensity to form and lead flocks of cruisers in various activities from ragtag racing regattas to isolated *ad hoc* island festivals.

Returning to city life in Santa Monica as the new millennium arrived, Tim captured the heart of his beloved bride Debby as she watched him trim the spinnaker on the downwind legs. They settled in to married life ashore with two cats and Tim's well-equipped garage study and workshop.

Advancing arthritis and spinal surgeries eventually limited sailing and racing activities, but the activity of writing expanded to fill the vacuum that Tim's nature abhors. After a couple of years supplying monthly columns to *the Marina Mariner magazine*, Tim tried his hand at illustrating his pieces in the offhand style he first admired as a elementary school student pouring through New Yorker cartoons of the fifties. For the readers who wonder where his childish line drawing style originated, the New Yorker cartoonists of that era are his models.

Tim Tunks has lots of racing and cruising experience. During the last forty years he has skippered hundreds of races and enjoyed a decade cruising the West Coast of Mexico. One highpoint was a most interesting month sailing, cruising, and diving from Tonga to Fiji on a 40-foot steel hulled junk-rigged boat with a lead line for depth sounding.

Playing his Padretimo role of sharing a vision for living an interesting life filled with curiosity and a sense of community, Tim offers this book as his Best Gift Ever to those who want a share of the gifts sailing bestowed on him.

To order additional copies of this book, or others in the series
The Best Gift Ever, go to www.thebestgiftever.info.

Bonus Pages

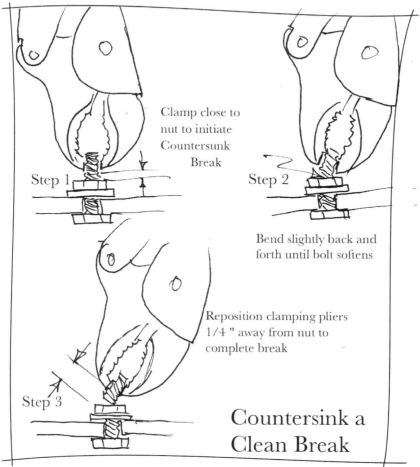

Clamp close to
nut to initiate
Countersunk
Break

Step 1

Step 2

Bend slightly back and
forth until bolt softens

Reposition clamping pliers
1/4 " away from nut to
complete break

Step 3

Countersink a
Clean Break

Make a Clean Break of It.

When deck hardware must be bolted through the cabin top, use this quick and easy method for trimming the bolt lengths flush with their nuts without grinding the sharp ends.

Utilize metal fatigue and the inherent bending weakness of a stainless bolt to make a controlled break at the desired place to countersink the slightly jagged bolt end within the nut. There are variations of this basic method, but I will teach the one I favor. You can easily learn this trick with a little experimentation and practice.

Master the technique by solidly securing a piece of scrap material through which you can fit a one-quarter inch stainless bolt. A piece of angle stock in your bench vise would be perfect but most any method of clamping your practice securely to bench, post, or what have you will suffice.

Fit the bolt through from the underside, place a washer under the nut on the topside, and tighten the nut securely. With Vise-Grip type locking pliers, clamp the excess bolt end and bend it back and forth gently until it breaks off. This will leave an unacceptable bit of sharp broken bolt end sticking out, however you will get a feeling for how little actual force is required to fatigue and break the threaded portion.

The skill you will acquire with practice is to position the break so the sharp broken bolt end is below the surface of the nut leaving nothing sharp sticking out—something I did not think possible until I saw it done.

Poco a poco is Spanish for "bit by bit", which is your key to clean breaking success.

Fit a new practice bolt and start making the first back and forth bends with the pliers locked quite close to the nut, restricting the bend to only a few degrees in each direction. Do this gently, bit by bit, to initiate the break inside the nut. (Note: If the fastener is not well tightened the bend can initiate on the wrong side of the nut, in which case that weakened bolt should be replaced.)

You will feel the metal start to soften with your gentle bending which is your signal to re-grip the bolt a quarter of an inch further from the nut, and, *poco a poco*, increase how far you bend in each direction. Soon you'll be rewarded with a clean break and nothing sticking beyond the nut.

If you want a custom finished look, make a BB sized ball of epoxy putty and work it into the nut's recess. (Epoxy putty in packaged ribbons or sticks is handy for all sorts of fast finish applications.)

If the deck hardware is to work under high loads, a double-thick nut can be substituted for a regular one to insure there will still be sufficient bolt threads remaining in the nut after the excess bolt has been removed. A little grinder work on a double thick nut to round off the exposed corners before installation will soften any future bumps or scrapes.

I find this technique superior to the use of "acorn nuts" which protrude about three times as far as double thick nuts, making acorns much more dangerous to any skull they contact.

Masthead View of Dinghy in Movies
(Note black box on side deck - It's a T-V)

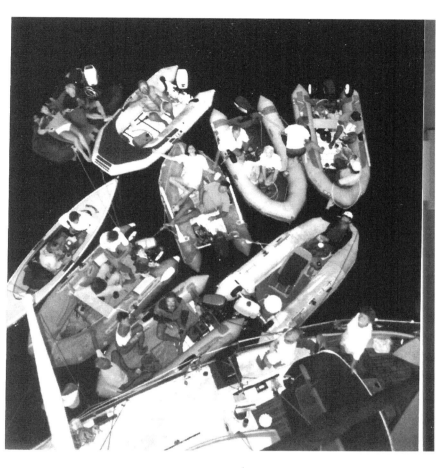

A major portion of cruising life's joy is making your own fun.

Stand Up Paddleboard Circa 1991

During Semana Santa (the Easter holiday in Mexico) the enginless Scallywag *would sail out to the uninhabited Marieta Islands in the mouth of Bahia Bandaras. to explore these volcanic islands with their huge population of blue footed boobies.*

We carried two Bic windsurfers and one kayak paddle which we put into service with a windsurfer mast substituting for the missing paddle.

Here was where I had my first encounter with giant manta rays.

Local Knowledge & Native Wisdom Getting over shyness is fun

Sailing with Guests Makes the Best Memories

Scallywag was the fifth boat hauled out of the water at Marina Seca in San Carlos, Sonora with their submersible hydraulic trailer. The boat yard did double duty, with cattle grazing there in the early morning. I hate to think how many harmful chemicals made it into their milk.

In the year 2000 Scallywag was loaded onto this same trailer to start her fourth trip North from Mexico—by land this time.

Scallywag with awnings in place enjoying the solitude of El Mogote, across the bay from La Paz. Mx. Developing easily deployed shade that could be quickly struck in sudden windstorms became a high art.

We joked of a contest named "The Awning Olympics." Imagine yourself sleeping soundly below when suddenly the breeze changes enough to wake you. At this point you have two minutes at most to get everything down before 40 kts. of wind hits you—and you are naked, can't find your glasses and have to urinate badly. That is the game.

Copied from a Puerta Vallarta newspaper showing *Scallywag* taking
first in class during the third *Regata de Bahia Banderas*

It seemed I could always find a racing fix when needed.

Scallywag carried a small staysail on an improvised Code "0" furling rig made from a small junked Mariner furling drum and swivel.

Encountering a sleeping finback whale cow asleep nursing her calf was a surprisingly spiritual event.

Difficult to appreciate from this B/W shot, these animals are huge and don't smell that good either.

This event happen near the beginning of my first year in Mexico and truly set the stage for the wonders to come.

I invite all you readers to visit www.thebestgiftever.info to see color versions of the photos in this book and lots more besides.

Fair winds, following seas, and may all your competition be good losers.

Santa Monica, CA
September 3. 2013

If you enjoyed my miscellany of stories and articles you can drop me a note at <padretimo@verizon.net>. With demand, I will hasten the production of Volume Two.

Too Busy Racing to Notice a Hitchiker

Made in the USA
San Bernardino, CA
27 September 2013